Roger Rosenblatt

LIFE ITSELF

Roger Rosenblatt has been an essayist for *Time* and a
columnist for *The Washington Post* and is currently
editor-at-large for *Life;* he is also the regular essayist for
The MacNeil/Lehrer NewsHour. Among his honors are
the Peabody and two George Polk awards. His *Children
of War*, translated into seven languages, won the 1983
Robert F. Kennedy Book Prize. He lives in New York
City.

ALSO BY ROGER ROSENBLATT

Witness

Children of War

Black Fiction

Roger Rosenblatt

LIFE ITSELF

Abortion in the American Mind

 *Vintage Books*

A Division of Random House, Inc.

New York

FIRST VINTAGE BOOKS EDITION, JANUARY 1993

Library of Congress Cataloging-in-Publication Data
Rosenblatt, Roger.
    Life itself: abortion in the American mind / Roger Rosenblatt.
      p. cm.
    Originally published: New York: Random House, 1992.
    Includes bibliographical references.
    ISBN 0-679-74373-1 (pbk.)
    1. Abortion—Political aspects—United States. I. Title.
HQ767.5.U5R67   1993
363.4'6—dc20   92-56377
             CIP

Manufactured in the United States of America
10 9 8 7 6 5 4 3 2 1

For Ginny, Carl, Amy, John, and Joannie,
my cherished family

Contents

Acknowledgments

I am deeply indebted to the following people, who contributed materially to this book and who much enlarged my understanding of the subject: Jennifer Wolff, whose imaginative and tireless research and reporting in Iowa and New York formed the basis for many of the book's ideas and conclusions; Temma Ehrenfeld, whose scrupulous study of the history of abortion and other relevant information was indispensable; Amy Bernstein, whose careful research and criticism got the book under way; Lisa Kaufman, a remarkably astute and challenging reader of the manuscript; Jane Freeman, who cheerfully typed the manuscript, and typed, and typed again, asking invaluable questions along the way.

Peter Osnos, a true book editor, brought to this work both sense and sensitivity, along with his considerable gifts for argument and organization.

Many conversations with friends and colleagues added to and, in some instances, shaped my thinking about the subject. For these I heartily thank Jim Autry and Sally Pedersen,

Derek and Sissela Bok, Ray Cave and Pat Ryan, Susan Chace, Mario Cuomo, Marian Wright Edelman, Walter and Elaine Goodman, Paul Gray, Peter Jennings, Joan Konner and Al Perlmutter, Stefan Kanfer, John and Jackie Leo, Jim and Kate Lehrer, Jay Lovinger, Sister Mary Paul and Sister Geraldine, Martin and Anne Peretz, Jack Rosenthal and Holly Russell, Michael Saltz, Stuart and Linda Schlesinger, Ron Shepard, Garry Trudeau and Jane Pauley, Virginia Walther, Alan Yepsen and Didi Weinblatt, Peter and Judy Weissman, David Yepson and Mary Stuart.

I am especially grateful to my brother, Peter Rosenblatt, for his thoughtful contributions to everything I write.

I am also indebted to Jim Gaines, my editor at *Life* magazine, who generously allowed me time to work on this project.

To Gloria Loomis, my friend and agent of seventeen years, my abiding thanks for her unfailing encouragement, her practical mind and good heart.

When I began to study abortion, many people whom I do not know were kind enough to send me their thoughts and points of view. They have my sincere gratitude, though I know that more than a few of them will not be pleased by my conclusions. I would also like to express appreciation to those who have written on abortion before me. If I have added a small amount to the understanding of this subject, it is because others added to mine.

Roger Rosenblatt

Preface to the Vintage Edition

Since this book originally appeared in March 1992, two note-worthy events have occurred in America's abortion wars, one specific, one general. The specific event—the 5–4 Supreme Court ruling in *Casey* v. *Planned Parenthood* in Pennsylvania in June—has caused the more dramatic reaction in public and in the press, but it may turn out to be the less significant. The general event—the acceleration of various movements to discover common ground on abortion—has evidenced itself little by little, incident by incident, but it may eventually establish the prevailing attitude toward abortion in America, thus shaping future laws. I hope that *Life Itself* has contributed to creating the atmosphere of common ground, but I take no credit for initiating that sort of thinking. As early as 1979, people on both sides of the issue have called for civilized discussions and conciliatory measures. I believe that my book simply came along at the moment when much of the country was ready to do what the book urges: learn to live with this issue, however uncomfortably, and move on to more pressing social problems.

Oddly, the *Casey* v. *Pennsylvania* decision, poorly conceived as it was, may also have contributed to an atmosphere of common ground by demonstrating that it is not possible to achieve common ground by whittling away at the rights guaranteed in *Roe* v. *Wade*. Whittling is what the *Casey* decision accomplished. Five justices stated that "the essential holding of *Roe* vs. *Wade* should be retained and once again reaffirmed." But the Court as a whole nonetheless supported the strictures sought by Pennsylvania. The majority held that a woman must be informed about fetal development and about alternatives to abortion; that a twenty-four-hour waiting period be imposed after she receives this information; that girls who are under the age of eighteen and unmarried must obtain the consent of their parents or a judge; that doctors keep records of their abortions; and that these records remain subject to public disclosure. The court struck down the requirement that women inform their husbands before they have an abortion.

Even if one considers the *Casey* v. *Pennsylvania* decision reasonable social policy, it makes for very bad law. The Court declared that anti-abortion laws must not pose an "undue burden" on women trying to obtain an abortion. Yet it also said that any measure that tries to get a woman to change her mind is constitutional. All this accomplishes is to deliver the matter to the caprice of individual judges.

The decision also throws the question back to the states. As this book argues, that has only led to a fractured national policy in which poor women are placed at a great disadvantage. The book urges that abortion laws be taken out of the Supreme Court, where they ought never to have been put in the first place, and that they should instead be settled by Congress. That suggestion has in fact been taken, though Congress has yet to shape an omnibus bill that would both preserve the framework of *Roe* and establish policies, such as sex education in public schools, that would make abortions less necessary.

Still, for all its flaws, the *Casey* v. *Pennsylvania* decision represented an effort to find a way for Americans to live with an issue we have been unable to live with for a quarter century. A more useful way to do this, as this book suggests, lies in embracing the uncompromisable elements in the issue rather than trying to create compromises that are false and destructive to both sides. In *Life Itself*, I offer the formula of "permit but discourage," which has been adopted by a number of commentators and was probably coined before me. To make that formula work, one must accept the fact that the great majority of the country wants to keep the terms of *Roe* v. *Wade* intact yet also disapproves of abortion as a practice. As the book also suggests, it is really not common ground the country ought to seek, but "uncommon ground."

For everyone concerned with this issue, it has been enormously gratifying to note the number of fair-minded and sympathetic discussions that have occurred recently. An activist group called Catholics for Free Choice has declared this the "year of dialogue." The Evangelical Lutheran Church issued a statement urging their congregations to "move beyond the usual 'pro-life' and 'pro-choice' language." Two years ago the director of the largest abortion clinic in St. Louis invited representatives of the pro-life movement to meet. "No one is ever going to convince me that it's all right to kill unborn babies," Loretto Wagner, the past president of Missouri Citizens for Life, said a few months ago. "But that doesn't mean we need to demonize each other. If [abortion] is not to become the Vietnam of the 1990s, we have to learn to sit down and talk to each other."

Apart from offering some theoretical and historical reasons

that abortion has so confounded American thinking, the encouragement of open discussion was my main objective in writing *Life Itself*. A country that has learned to accept and absorb contrary attitudes on a variety of important social issues could, I felt, include abortion among them. Since the book's publication, I have received long, thoughtful letters from a considerable number of readers who found in the book a catalyst for expressing what had been inexpressible for them before. In the hands of these people, and of millions now beginning to talk this subject out, lies the future of abortion in America.

As I write this prefatory note, Bill Clinton has just been elected president. Both Bill and Hillary Clinton are advocates of parental notification—a problematic compromise on abortion, yet one that represents a way for most Americans to live with the practice. With the Clintons in the White House, a movement toward common uncommon ground will almost certainly continue to gain strength. Perhaps as soon as a year from now, as a result of open discussions, the national attitude of permit-but-discourage will be established, and on that attitude Congress can build a law that speaks the people's minds and hearts. Then we can live with one another again.

Roger Rosenblatt
November 4, 1992

LIFE ITSELF

Chapter 1

Where We Are

*T*he veins in his forehead bulged so prominently they might have been blue worms that had worked their way under the surface of his skin. His eyes bulged, too: The pupils dilated to make them appear entirely black; capillaries zigzagged in all directions, like the red tails of flares. His face was pulled tight about the jaw, which thrust forward like a snowplow attachment on the grille of a truck. From the flattened *O* of his mouth, the word *murderer* erupted in a regular rhythm, the repetition of the *r*'s giving the word the sound of an outboard motor that had failed to catch.

She, for her part, paced up and down directly in front of him, saying nothing. Instead, she held high a large cardboard sign on a stick, showing the cartoonish drawing of a bloody coat hanger over the caption NEVER AGAIN. Like his, her face was taut with fury, her lips pressed together so tightly they folded under and vanished, making her mouth appear a raw wound. Whenever she drew close to him, she would deliberately lower the sign and turn it toward him, so that he would be yelling his *murderer* at the picture of the coat hanger.

For nearly twenty years these two have been at each other with all the hatred they can unearth. Sometimes the man is a woman, sometimes the woman a man. They are black, white, Hispanic, Asian; they make their homes in Missouri or New Jersey; they are teenagers and pharmacists and college professors, Catholic, Baptist, Jew. They have exploded at each other on the steps of the Capitol in Washington, D.C., in front of abortion clinics, hospitals and politicians' homes, on village greens and the avenues of cities. Their rage is tireless; at every decision of the U.S. Supreme Court or of the President or of the state legislatures, it rises like a missile seeking only the heat of its counterpart.

This is where America is these days on the matter of abortion, or where it seems to be. In fact, it is very hard to tell how the country really feels about abortion, because those feelings we learn about are almost always the ones displayed in political arenas. If one were to go by the amount of noise generated every time a pro- or anti-abortion decision is published, one might conclude that Americans are seething constantly over the issue. Yet most people, unless their families are directly involved in the choice of an abortion, do not argue about it. The arguing has been left to those who have a political stake in the subject, and even they do their "arguing" in the streets.

Most people do not speak of abortion at all. Friends who gladly debate other volatile issues—political philosophy, war, race—shy away from abortion. The problem is too private, too personal, too bound up with one's faith or spiritual identity. Give abortion five seconds of thought, and it quickly spirals down in the mind to the most basic questions about human life, to the mysteries of birth and our relationship with our souls. It is difficult to disentangle, much less express, the feelings it engenders. For whatever reasons, we simply will not talk about the subject with one another unless, of course, "we" agree on one particular position, and even then, more is inferred from habitual attitudes than is actually discussed. We will march in demonstrations, shout and carry placards, vote in a national election where abortion is an issue, but we will not talk about it.

This book is an attempt to encourage a discussion about abortion, by which the country may deal honestly and openly with the issue, may learn to accept, however uncomfortably, the practice of abortion as part of American life and find a way to move ahead to other social problems that could profit from the country's undivided attention. The book also suggests that the very discussion of our private feelings on abortion may constitute a resolution of the problem. Since the abortion issue can never be resolved completely—since, logically, there is no common ground on which those who condemn the practice as murder will stand with those who do not, or who will accept "murder" in this context—the resolution, it seems to me, lies in learning to live with the irreconcilable. That may begin to be achieved by saying what we feel, in all its emotional contradictions.

I think we have to learn to live on "uncommon ground" in the matter of abortion; that we must not only accept but embrace a state of tension that requires a tolerance of ambivalent feelings, respect for different values and sensibilities, and no small amount of compassion. In the fourth and final chapter, I will try to show that this uncommon ground is within reach.

The book has been divided into four stages that I hope lead reasonably to the proposition that Americans must and in fact are ready to live with abortion as an irreconcilable problem.

This first chapter is meant to establish where we are in the debate. Where Americans really are on abortion is, I believe, a quite different place from that which the public activities on the matter would indicate. The public face the country puts on abortion would strongly suggest that we are at a hopeless impasse. I believe the opposite: that we are more prepared than we realize to reach a resolution, and if we begin to vent our mixed feelings on the subject, the resolution will be at hand. Most Americans are both for the choice of abortion as a principle and against abortion itself—for themselves. To state that ambivalence is to begin to deal with it.

Chapter 2 offers a history of the subject in which America's anguish over abortion is seen to be anomalous. The four thousand-year-old history of abortion from the an-

cients to the present shows a recurrence of certain fundamental questions as well as the ways various cultures have
sought to answer them. When we come to America in this
history, especially contemporary history, we see a country that, unlike the civilizations before it or around it, has
been thrown for a loop by abortion. You might think that
one look at this history would have taught our country
that there is no clear-cut solution to the problem, thus
ambivalence would seem to be an acceptable posture. Yet
America seems unable to learn, much less to act on, that
lesson. This is doubly curious given the fact that there are
so many other troublesome issues, such as free speech,
with which we live ambivalently all the time. Abortion,
clearly, is something else.

In Chapter 3 I suggest some reasons why abortion has
confounded America so deeply. Our particular and peculiar history, with its origins both in the Puritans' concept
of the City on the Hill and its subterranean secular religion, has created national characteristics that have
become explosive when touched by abortion. American
individualism, American optimism, our preoccupation
with evil, our dogged middle-classness, especially as regards sexuality and the role of women—all are agitated by
the controversy. In a way, America is a setup for the
abortion issue. Every basic idea the country holds, however benign in itself, turns volatile in this context.

Since this is so, how can we resolve this irresolvable
issue and move on to some social concerns that *can* be
resolved? That is the subject of Chapter 4, in which I look
at the state of Iowa as a model of how we might both
discuss the complications of abortion and find a reason-

ably satisfactory attitude on the subject. Here, with the concrete illustration of a state and the opinions of its citizens, I test the proposition offered in Chapter 1, that we must accept irresolution on this issue and that we are ready to do it. In Iowa's balance of private values and community obligations, I believe, lies a way for the majority of the country as a whole both to live with abortion and to strive to live without it.

To begin to get to that point, however, to where we can eventually be, I return in the present chapter to "where we are" now. And as already noted, this is a much more complicated place than where the public argument would indicate.

~~~~

Seventy-three percent of Americans polled in 1990 were in favor of abortion rights. Yet 77 percent in another poll said they regard abortion as a form of murder (see Note, page 184). One has to know nothing else to realize how conflicted a moral problem we have before and within us.

The fact that abortion entails conflict, however, does not mean that most of us do not know how we feel about it. People certainly know how they feel about abortion when the question of having one involves friends or family; even in situations where abortion is a clear necessity, no one much likes it. I believe that the great majority of Americans not only acknowledge these contradictory feelings but, political appearances to the contrary notwithstanding, are prepared to live with them. Up to now that acknowledgment has been a sort of tentative internal exercise, perhaps because most people do not realize how widespread feelings of conflict are. Yet occasionally they surface. Many women staunchly defend abortion rights politically but say they would never choose the option themselves. If more pro-life advocates were aware of that ambivalence, or if more pro-choice advocates made an effort to express it, that alone might offer a ground on which opponents could begin to edge toward an acceptable understanding.

My own attitude toward abortion is similarly conflicted—that is, my political position does not begin to cover my range of feelings on the matter. I ought to state that position up front, however, so that the point of view from which this book is written is clear and so that I can get my politics, which plays but one part in my attitude, out of the way.

My stand on abortion is conventionally pro-choice: Every woman in America, in my opinion, ought to have the legal right to choose an abortion, and abortion ought to be funded by the government so that poor women are not put at an additional disadvantage. I do not believe that any satisfactory practical compromise may be applied to this position; the modifications of parental consent or parental notification, now the law in several states, seem to me only to whittle away at a woman's—that is, an American's—basic private freedom of choice.

I do not believe that a clear-cut intellectual or moral compromise is available to the issue, either. If abortion is considered murder, I do not see how it can ever be entirely acceptable to those who oppose it, even though they may allow certain exceptions to the rule. If it is not considered murder, on what grounds would those who favor abortion rights want them restricted?

Nor do I believe that the question of when life begins, over which there is so much scientific and spiritual haggling, is pertinent or useful to the debate. I would be perfectly willing to concede that life begins at conception, yet I would still advocate a system in which the killing of an unborn child is preferable to forcing an unwilling mother to give birth.

And I do not believe that community rights in this matter are equal to individual rights. While the rights of the community are not to be ignored, the final decision should be the individual woman's, no matter how misguided she may be thought or how strongly the rest of society disapproves.

I feel almost foolish stating the above because, though I believe the pro-choice position to be right, this book is not a pro-choice argument. I do not even like the terms *pro-choice* and *pro-life*, though I will use them for convenience. The terms, imprecise in themselves, are ideological constructions, invented to keep abortion in the realm of confrontational politics rather than allowing it to be discussed rationally and sympathetically by ordinary people.

For the past twenty years, abortion has existed mainly as a shouting match that has been overheard by ordinary people. I believe we need a discussion in which ordinary people can recognize their own thoughts and feelings and in which we can also recognize one another.

By where we are on abortion I mean where we are as a country, and as I have suggested, that is not where we appear to be. To go by the political picture—that is, the legislative bills introduced and/or passed in the states since the *Webster* decision of 1989—the country is hopelessly divided into two camps. Yet the movement in the states since *Webster* is the product of sophisticated, organized political effort and gives no sign that it is the consequence of genuine feeling on the part of citizens.

The *Webster* decision arose under the following circumstances:

In July 1989, the Bush administration, acting through the Department of Justice, asked the Supreme Court to overturn *Roe* v. *Wade*. The *Roe* decision, handed down on January 22, 1973, had determined that a woman had the absolute right to choose an abortion during the first trimester. *Webster* (*Webster* v. *Reproductive Health Systems*) involved a Missouri statute found unconstitutional by federal courts. The Missouri legislature stated that life begins at conception. It banned the use of public employees and facilities for abortions and required a test for fetal viability in and after the twentieth week of pregnancy. The Supreme Court upheld the Missouri statute but did not overturn *Roe* v. *Wade*.

In amicae briefs, pro-life groups argued that the *Roe* trimester system did not reflect changes in medical technology that make it possible to save younger fetuses. Pro-choice groups, on the other hand, noted that the same advances make abortions safer to perform later in pregnancy.

The state of Missouri argued in its brief that the trimester approach should be shelved because its determination of viability is arbitrary and "that the state has a compelled interest in protecting [fetal] life through all stages of pregnancy." The Justice Department asked the Court to overturn *Roe* and return the authority to regulate abortion to the states in the first trimester. Reproductive Health Systems, on the other side, argued that "legal safe abortion is a choice exercised by one of every four pregnant women in the United States."

Chief Justice William Rehnquist, in an opinion joined by Justice Byron White and Justice Anthony Kennedy, concluded that the government has an interest in protecting life throughout pregnancy, thus justifying the Missouri testing requirement. The justices, moreover, voted to overturn *Roe*. Justice Antonin Scalia argued separately for overturning *Roe*, accusing the Court of cowardice in not doing so. "It appears that the mansion of constitutionalized abortion law, constructed overnight in *Roe* v. *Wade*," said Scalia, "must be disassembled door-jamb by door-jamb, and never entirely brought down, no matter how wrong it may be."

Justice Harry Blackmun, in an opinion joined by justices William Brennan and Thurgood Marshall, argued that the Missouri statute violated the right to an abortion established in *Roe*. In a third opinion, Justice John Paul Stevens declared the testing requirements unconstitutionally burdensome even in the absence of a special abortion right. Justice Sandra Day O'Connor said the

Missouri testing requirement did not impose an "undue burden" on abortion decisions.

The Court's decision, leaving *Roe* tottering but not yet fallen, amounted to an open invitation to state legislatures to test how far they could regulate abortion. Many states accepted that invitation eagerly, with the resulting impression that the country was about to overturn *Roe* v. *Wade* before the Court got to it again and establish an America where abortion is effectively prohibited.

Where we really are on the matter of abortion is, I believe, a quite different place from where the states' activity since *Webster* would suggest we are. I might say parenthetically that where we *were* as a country prior to *Webster* was a quite different place from where *Roe* v. *Wade* suggested we were as well. Had that not been so, the current state of high turmoil would probably not exist; it has been building dramatically in people's minds since *Roe* v. *Wade*. Right or wrong, *Roe* v. *Wade* had all the effect of a law without emerging from the popular consensus that ought to go into a law. I do not think I am alone among liberals in feeling that one of the troubles wrought by *Roe* v. *Wade* was the misidentification of abortion as purely a rights issue. If more liberals at the time had appreciated that doing right was as important as exercising rights, that the emotions of anti-abortion Americans were not only valid but to a great extent shared, the process of national healing might have begun sooner.

These political events following *Webster* have been misleading in themselves. Anyone following the issue on television or in the papers in recent years would reasonably believe that the country has been heading pell-mell toward a severely restrictive pro-life position. That is not so. The country has been heading in both the pro-life and the pro-choice directions simultaneously and equally, which does not make for fewer problems, only different ones.

What the *Webster* decision in fact did was to allow the polar divisions on the issue to establish themselves in the open. By weakening *Roe* v. *Wade*, *Webster* could have encouraged the sort of popular discussion that might have aided the resolution of the issue, but instead of discussion, the states responded with one set of laws or another. Thus the importance of *Webster* was simply to permit the states to make their own terms and to create their own versions of national law.

If one looks at all the states' political activity since *Webster*, the picture that develops is of a country not changing its mind about abortion but fortifying both its minds, and growing farther and more adamantly apart. The amount and variety of pro-life movement in the states has increased enormously and in some instances with much drama. But the pro-choice activity has also intensified. For all the state bills to delimit abortion rights in recent years, the legislatures in twenty-two states adjourned in 1991 either without enacting any abortion restrictions or having defeated all abortion-related bills for the 1991 session. Thirty-four states have actually solidified their pro-choice positions since *Webster*. In January 1991, there were more state governors openly declared as supporting legal abortion than there had been in June 1989, before *Webster*. Similarly, more state legislatures, both houses, supported abortion rights in January 1991 than they had two years earlier.

In spite of this activity and in spite of the fact that most Americans want choice, the right to choose is at greater risk than before. That apparent contradiction can begin to be explained by taking an overview of bills introduced since *Webster* and by noting their general tendency. As of May 30, 1991, forty-nine state legislatures had convened their sessions. At least 220 bills restricting abortion had been introduced in at least forty-five states.

Bills imposing anti-abortion counseling requirements and/or mandatory delays have been introduced in at least twenty-one states. On March 28, 1991, the Mississippi legislature voted to override Governor Ray Mabus's veto of an anti-abortion counseling measure in that state. On April 1, 1991, Governor George Sinner, of North Dakota, signed an anti-abortion counseling measure into law. Similar measures are expected in at least two other states, Maine and Wisconsin.

Bills to limit use of public funds, facilities, or employees for the performance of abortions have been introduced in at least twelve states. Bills to require married women to gain consent from or notify their husbands before having an abortion or to allow a man to prevent an abortion have been introduced in at least five states. Bills to prohibit abortion for "sex selection" have been introduced in at least ten states. Bills to require viability testing before performing an abortion have been introduced in at least seven states.

Bills intended to ban virtually all abortions have been introduced in at least fourteen state legislatures—in Alabama, Indiana, Louisiana, Maryland, Mississippi, Missouri, North Dakota, Rhode Island, South Carolina, South Dakota, and Texas. On January 25, 1991, Governor Norman Bangerter, of Utah, signed a ban on abortion into law. On April 1, 1991, Governor George Sinner, of North Dakota, vetoed a bill that would have banned virtually all abortions in that state; the legislature sustained the veto. Alabama, Minnesota, and Oklahoma may face ballot issues on the question of banning most abortions.

Bills to limit young women's access to abortion by requiring the consent or notification of parents have been introduced in twenty-three states. Similar measures are expected to be introduced in at least four others—Illinois, Maine, Nevada, and Oregon. While thirty-five states have laws preventing minors from obtaining an abortion without parental consent, only fifteen of those laws are enforced.

The introduction of these abortion-related bills (and there have been others with different purposes) has been the product of two connected phenomena. One, as mentioned earlier, is the effective and intensified work of the pro-life movements in the states. Before *Webster*, pro-life activists behaved more like guerrilla fighters than a political organization. With the invitation to opposition that *Webster* afforded, these groups began to make openly clear to state legislators that their careers might depend on following the pro-life line.

As for the state legislators themselves, before *Webster* they had been free to wear at least two faces in public with regard to abortion. As long as *Roe* was secure, the ardently pro-choice legislators had no cause to come out vociferously in support of abortion rights and could more profitably remain mum on the issue, so as not to offend unnecessarily those who disagreed. Those who waffled on abortion rights or who opposed them either a lot or a little could manage to appear to be obeying the law while restraining their passions to repeal it. In other words, as long as *Roe* was in place, the legislators on all sides could hide from the issue while at the same time suggest to all sides that they concurred with everybody—a politician's heaven.

No sooner did the *Webster* decision come down than these same legislators were suddenly exposed to the light. Now, both those who supported and those who opposed abortion rights had to declare themselves or risk being voted out of office. Few of the legislators wanted to abolish abortion wholesale. But many more saw in the proposal of such restrictive measures as parental consent and parental notification ideal compromises that would allow them to tilt pro-life without toppling over. By supporting such restrictions, the lawmakers could appear to be advocating "good ideas" without bearing the responsibility of making abortion illegal.

There is another important factor that contributes to endangering abortion rights. While many states have reaffirmed their support of those rights, they have also seen a steep decline in the number of places where abortions are available. Over thirty states have experienced that decline. In South Dakota there is but one doctor who continues to provide abortions, and the one such doctor in all of western Iowa recently gave up the practice. Now women in that half of the state find it necessary to seek abortions in Nebraska or travel east to Des Moines or Iowa City. Many poor women are not able to afford the trip.

This decline has come about largely but not wholly because of the efforts of the pro-life movement. Continuous demonstrations in front of abortion clinics, hospitals, and even the homes of doctors who provide abortions have, over the years, made it too uncomfortable for many to persevere in the practice. For some doctors this has meant having to forfeit money, since abortions can be lucrative. But they have not found the turmoil worth it. For others it has meant giving up providing a service in whose moral value they deeply believe. Some, too, have simply stopped for personal or professional reasons.

In all cases the result has been damaging to abortion rights. It means little to a woman that she is legally allowed an abortion if she can find no place to get one. This decline of abortion providers rarely makes the news, but it is just as effective an instrument of change as the laws in Louisiana and Utah.

Yet more damaging to the possible resolution of the problem as a whole, in my view, is that the political schism has been solidified. The *Webster* decision forced both individual politicians and political bodies to take firm sides on abortion. With the matter apparently about to be thrown from the Supreme Court to the states, each state became a potential nation in terms of its permissions and prohibitions. The pro-choice and pro-life activists who found it unwieldy to exert their influence over the country as a whole saw in the individual states a much more manageable situation. Those running for office in the states regarded themselves, or were told to regard themselves, as little presidents in charge of a people's rights and morals.

As for the "big," the real, presidency, it is interesting how the new situation has served it. On the one hand, presidential candidates in 1992, for the first time ever, may have to declare themselves as openly on abortion as have state legislators. On the other hand, they may choose to express feelings with deliberate vagueness and get away with that on the grounds that abortion is likely to become a states issue entirely in which the president has no business interfering. President Bush, initially pro-choice, has already established himself as pro-life. That alone, of course, will make it extremely difficult for the Democratic candidate to veil his or her views.

The presidency aside, our country's political position is openly and patently split. That gap grows larger, deeper, and clearer and is likely to continue to do so until or unless Americans find a way to express themselves on abortion more directly to one another and with fewer slogans and more nuance and common sympathy. That, of course, is not the way of politics.

~~~~

You would think that the public intellectual discussion of abortion would be more satisfying than the political activity. Yet where we are in the public debate over abortion is much the same place as the politics, since the public argument seems only to constitute the verbal basis of the political activity. There has been an enormous number of articles and columns on abortion since *Webster,* some very thoughtful and inventive, but none, as far as I can tell, has affected the way the public debate on the subject is constructed or presented. At least forty-four books on abortion have appeared since *Webster,* a great many promoting one side or the other; they have not enlarged the argument. Books on legal aspects of the question, such as Laurence H. Tribe's *The Clash of Absolutes* or personal testimonies such as *The Choices We Made: Twenty-five Women Speak Out on Abortion,* edited by Angela Bonavoglia, have added much to the understanding of abortion but have not been absorbed in open discussions. Those discussions remain largely as they have been from the start, an exhibition of polar views.

This was demonstrated most clearly in an ABC television forum in September, 1990, moderated by Peter Jennings, the purpose of which was to gather the principal antagonists on the issue in a single place and see what grounds there might be for compromise or new thinking.

In spite of Jennings's responsible and diligent pursuit of those goals, they did not materialize. The event revealed less about abortion than about how the argument had calcified into predictable stands and poses.

I apologize for giving what may, at first, seem an overlong account of the Jennings forum, but you will see how the responses of the panelists broke down into two camps of argument in spite of the variety of backgrounds and professional perspectives. The two camps were, as ever, "choice" and "life." Occasionally, discussion would produce something other than those polar ideas, but no sooner would a tug toward a middle ground be felt than each side would revert to its traditional posture.

The full extent of the abortion dilemma was on display that night. The main participants were: Faye Wattleton, president of Planned Parenthood; Judge Robert Bork, the defeated Reagan nominee for the Supreme Court; Richard Wirthlin, a pollster; Kate Michelman, executive director of the National Abortion Rights Action League (NARAL); Mary Cunningham Agee, executive director of the Nurturing Network, an organization that helps and advises women with unwanted pregnancies who choose not to have abortions; Dr. Jane Hodgson, an obstetrician who had participated in or performed over thirty thousand abortions; the Reverend Bobby Welch, a Florida TV minister and pastor of the First Baptist Church in Daytona Beach; Linda Bird Francke, a strongly pro-choice writer, who was running for the New York State Assembly from eastern Long Island; Dr. John Willke, president of the National Right to Life Committee (NRLC); Olivia Gans, director of American Victims of Abortion; and the Reverend Richard McBrien, chairman of the theology department at the University of Notre Dame. I participated in the role of a writer and a citizen trying to understand the subject.

The most effective speakers were Ms. Wattleton, whose regal appearance cooperated with her near perfectly formed sentences; Judge Bork, who has a rich voice and who, with his cotton-tuft beard, looked like an Amish farmer; Pastor Welch, who had the manner of a pepper-pot shortstop and talked with the Southwestern cadences of most TV ministers; Olivia Gans, whose zealotry could be read in the insistent innocence of her face; and Father McBrien. McBrien always talked calmly and was one of the few participants who seemed to be working out his thoughts on the spot.

Except for Francke, no politician running in the primary elections being held on the Tuesday following the broadcast had agreed to come on the show. Francke's opponent for the New York Assembly, John Behan, had evidently said he would appear, but he never showed up, and the chair that had been reserved for him remained vacant throughout the program. (On Tuesday, Francke lost to Behan by a margin of 3 to 1.) Governor Mario Cuomo had been invited but declined; even for Cuomo, a shoo-in for reelection and one of the few major politicians in the country with an articulated and sophisticated position on abortion, the issue was deemed politically perilous.

The panelists sat in a circular theater with a gleaming black floor and a black-and-chrome look to it; the set suggested excessively modern, all-business severity. We were arranged in a sort of horseshoe, roughly according to political positions. As Jennings faced the panelists from the open end of the horseshoe, those to his left were pro-choice, with the exception of Father McBrien; those to his right, pro-life. In the middle, directly opposite Jennings, in a cluster of three, sat Judge Bork, Mary Cunningham Agee, and I. I guessed that I was to occupy that middle ground, which did not exist.

Jennings began with the question "Is abortion a civil war?" Most everyone agreed that it was, with Pastor

Welch giving the most colorful definition of a civil war—
"where the nation divides on an issue and begins to
struggle with itself and people choose sides and end up on
one of the sides or other and get banged around and
bruised up and [there's] a lot of injury within one nation.
That's a civil war."

Bork quibbled with the term: "I think it's a deeply
divisive issue, but we have a number of deeply divisive
issues in this country."

Kate Michelman broadened the question: "I think it's
a very important issue and I think that there are a lot of
emotions. I think that the American public, though, is
ready for this country to finally address what the real
issue is, which is the high number of unintended pregnancies. Rather than fighting about whether a woman
should have the right to make the decision once she faces
a crisis pregnancy, the American public is hungry for a
national policy that's coherent and cohesive, that works
to prevent the need for abortion, that ends infant mortality, that emphasizes sex education and sexuality education. I mean, we could do a lot more than fight about
abortion . . ."

At this point, Jennings interrupted Michelman and
asked "what abortion means" to various panelists.

Dr. Willke responded: "It is a simple fact, proven for
more than a hundred years, that what grows within the
mother is living, is human, is already a boy or a girl, is
complete and intact already at the first-cell stage. This is
a human life growing within her. When you destroy this
human life, the accurate biologic word for this is *kill*.
Abortion kills an embryonic baby. Now, we don't kill

one-year-old girls who walk at their mother's side. We don't kill thirty-year-old people. The government stops us from doing that, and that's a legitimate role of government. We don't think that we should kill two-month-old little girls who just happen to still live in the womb."

Welch and Olivia Gans nodded vehemently.

Dr. Hodgson countered that she did not think abortion constituted killing at all. The obstetrician said, "I think I have done a humane service for lots of women in this world. I don't look upon [abortion] as killing, because I do not consider that any embryo or fetus is a person. It is a potential person."

Faye Wattleton added, "Well, I think that the opposition to a woman choosing the option of abortion will certainly label us many things, but we know very much that the killer of women is illegal abortion and that is why we believe that women should have a choice. And then I would agree with Kate that if we dislike this as much as the individuals who have spoken ahead of us say that they do, then they should join with us in helping to reduce the incidence of unintended pregnancy."

"The fundamental moral issue," said Bork, "is whether or not what's being killed is a human being. And I don't think that people who describe themselves as pro-choice, if they believed it were a human being, would say, 'We choose to kill it.' I think they don't believe it's a human being."

Ms. Wattleton responded, "I don't believe that a single one of us does not believe that a fetus is a living fetus; we are not suggesting that it is some inanimate object. The question is, when you have a woman's life and her needs and her health on the one side and the developing fetus on the other, a choice has to be made. And that choice should be left to the individual."

Thus the major, and traditional, battle line was drawn in the debate—between the value of the right to choose and the value of the unborn life. It would have helped the forum if that line had been pursued, but the Bork-Wattleton exchange was followed by a useless, if oddly entertaining, digression in the person of Ms. Gans.

American Victims of Abortion, which Ms. Gans directs, was created out of the experience of Ms. Gans's own abortion at the age of twenty-two. Because she deeply regretted that decision, which she said she made at the insistence of her boyfriend, she later founded her organization, the purpose of which is to advise women with unwanted pregnancies how to keep their babies. Ms. Gans is a foe of Planned Parenthood, which, she said, had misled her toward abortion as her sole option. Ms. Wattleton interrupted, insisting that the practice of Planned Parenthood is to advise women on the full range of options available, abortion being but one. The two of them went back and forth, with Ms. Gans finally becoming so irritating in not giving up the floor to anyone else that Jennings, ordinarily the model of courtesy, deliberately stepped between Ms. Gans and the camera in an effort to shut her up.

For a while, it looked as if the entire direction of the forum was to be swung in the direction of Ms. Gans. Ms. Francke observed that Ms. Gans appeared to "fit a certain sort of personality" in her effort to redeem herself after being "coerced" into her abortion. And Ms. Gans would seize several opportunities to repeat remarks about her aborted "baby" and her regretted decision.

Mary Cunningham Agee addressed Ms. Gans's former plight by describing the work of her own Nurturing Network: "If Olivia came to our offices, we would let her know that if she chose to give birth to her child, we would be prepared to provide her with a doctor who would take care of the entire expenses—either the doctor or we would; a counselor that she could meet with as frequently as she needed to during and immediately after her pregnancy; a nurturing home with whom she could live if her own home was no longer available with her parents or her boyfriend. We would give her, most importantly, if she's in college, an opportunity to transfer to a different college so that peer pressure would not be an issue. If she's a working woman, we'd give her a comparable job in a different environment. . . . We would give her a job in a different location where she could take a leave of absence from her current employer, if this is necessary, and continue her career path."

All this won the hearty applause of the audience, though to me Mrs. Agee's network sounded a bit like the government's federal witness protection program.

So much was said by Ms. Gans, Mrs. Agee, and then by Dr. Willke about what Planned Parenthood did and did not advise women to do that an exasperated Ms. Wattleton finally protested: "Mr. Jennings, I don't think that this program was designed as a referendum on Planned Parenthood."

Then Ms. Wattleton added: "I think the point is—to

really get at why we are concerned about this issue—is that people do have a wide divergence, in a pluralistic society, of opinions. We seek moral guidance from our religious teachers, not from politicians or people who want to meddle in our lives. And that's really what the essence of this system of democracy in government and our pluralistic society is about. We only plead that we be permitted—the 'muddled middle,' the people who are confused, the people who are conflicted, and Americans are conflicted about this issue—to be left to our own devices to work these things out for ourselves in our own lives." That, too, won much applause, but no further conversation.

Until Father McBrien spoke, nothing much of substance was said after that. Father McBrien made the necessary point, which ran counter to the forum's premise, that abortion was playing "a relatively minor role" in the upcoming primary elections. He elaborated on the significance of other national issues—taxes, the deficit, congressional leadership—to the voters. He said that for himself, he was "dismayed" that abortion was not being taken as seriously as it ought to be.

He stated, too, that as a Catholic he believed abortion "immoral." And yet, he said, American Catholics also have to respect the lack of consensus about the issue in our society. "Therefore our laws have to reflect that [lack of consensus]."

At that point, Father McBrien and Pastor Welch got into an unproductive if excited exchange about how an individual could be at once pro-choice and a Christian, with both men talking past each other from opposite sides of the circle and Welch referring confidently to his direct conversations with God.

But what Father McBrien had said about the consequences of living in a society without a consensus on abortion was potentially the most helpful remark made by anyone that night. To me this was the most important moment of the evening, though later I came to feel that America does have a consensus on abortion that remains unspoken. What impressed me about Father McBrien was his clarity on his position as a clergyman in America. His personal and religious morality forbade his approving of abortion in any situation, but even in this he was willing to accept his role as an American citizen, which requires people to live with several things they dislike.

The forum concluded, way beyond the original ninety minutes allotted to it, with Jennings asking the participants if we thought that people would still be arguing over this issue five years from then.

Ms. Francke: "Oh, I certainly hope not. No, the emphasis should be on the living, caring for those children and families that we already have."

Rev. McBrien: "I hope not, too. I think the only way out of it is the way that Kate Michelman and Governor Mario Cuomo and others have pointed to. We've got to eliminate the causes of unwanted pregnancies, and if we can work together, liberals and conservatives, religious people and nonreligious people alike, to eliminate the reasons why young women feel that they must have an abortion when they don't want to have an abortion, then we can, together, do something constructive and stop this useless and endless debate about whether there's a baby there with a personality or whether or not it's simply a woman's right."

Dr. Willke: "Abortion is either killing the child or you let the baby live. There isn't much in between. What we have to do here is recognize this as a basic civil and human rights issue. We're killing every third baby conceived in America; 43 percent of the abortions are now repeat abortions; 98 percent are done for social and economic reasons. We're trying to solve all kinds of social and economic problems by the ghastly violence of killing our kids. We're going to be discussing this same thing in five years. We can't continue this ghastly violence."

Ms. Wattleton: "I think that first of all, the American people are tired of this discussion in politics and in the public arena, and we would like to be left alone to decide for ourselves. The American people want us to shut up in the public arena on this issue and turn to the question of prevention of pregnancy and not punishment of women."

Dr. Hodgson: "I think that technology is going to answer a lot of these questions. The technology is moving faster all the time. We are learning new methods of reproduction and new birth control pills and the RU-486 will probably be introduced, in addition to contraceptive research. We have to consider the fetal tissue research that's going on and the genetic research that's going on. The advances in technology will be amazing in the next decade or so."

Ms. Gans: "The people of the United States have the right to decide this question because we are the government. It's a sensitive issue because it does involve caring for women in a just and honorable way and the dignity of their children as well. Both of them have a dignity that must be protected. We as Americans who have the power of the vote must use that to both protect the children and also provide for their families, including their mothers, in the most immediate way. I think we definitely will be discussing this until we recognize that we cannot continue with a million and a half abortions every year. We have to resolve the issues for women, but not by killing their children. And until we solve that, we will be nowhere."

Pastor Welch: "I think it'll be altogether different in five years. I believe that *Roe* v. *Wade* will definitely be overturned in five years. Things are going to change; it's going to become a more pro-life environment five years from now."

Ms. Michelman: "Well, I think we've demonstrated here tonight that this is an extraordinarily complicated issue involving lots of moral and religious and philosophical questions, and I think if we don't start focusing on the real problem, which is one that we've mentioned over and over—the unintended pregnancy rate, the lack of contraception or more effective contraception, the lack of sex education—we are going to continue to have this debate, but we're focused on the wrong thing. I do think that the attempt to restrict abortion is part of a much larger societal trend to control and even punish women. I think there *will* be a civil war if *Roe* v. *Wade* is overturned, by the way."

Judge Bork: "I don't think [the debate] ever will [end]. I think it may become less of a civil war if *Roe* v. *Wade* is overturned. That was the point at which this thing became an inflammatory national issue, because one side of the debate was ruled out of order by the Supreme Court. If we can overturn *Roe* v. *Wade,* then we can continue the process of discussion and debate and adjustment of the laws. A moral debate will then take place within the American public and the kinds of things we've been discussing here will be the kinds of things people will come to understand."

Jennings wound up the discussion, saying, "I must confess, when we started this program I thought of discovering common ground at the beginning and decided that there was going to be none, so at least from this reporter's point of view, I'm glad to hear you say so."

He graciously gave me the final word. I said I thought that it would be madness if five years from now we had a patchwork of different abortion laws depending on what state of the union you happened to live in. I also agreed lamely that common ground might be found. But that was merely my way of closing the remarks and steering clear of trouble. Common ground was not the same thing as learning to live with uncommon ground, and everything I had heard that night had reconfirmed my impression that the kind of compromises required by abortion would not be susceptible to standard negotiations.

Most of the thorny aspects of the abortion issue were not even mentioned during the forum. No one brought up the question of legal exceptions made in cases of rape and incest. No one raised the idea of parental consent and/or notification—though proposals along those lines were gaining strength in many states. No one spoke of the myriad of ethical riddles brought up by new reproductive technology.

Here's a question I was tempted to raise but did not: Women taking new fertility drugs usually produce five or six eggs, of which two or three at most can survive. The procedure for getting rid of the extra embryos is euphemistically called selective reduction. But it's simply an abortion at an early stage. My question to pro-life advocates would have been: Would you approve of this type of abortion in such cases, since some lives would be saved even as others were lost?

Here's a question I might have put to pro-choice advocates: A basic tenet of pro-choice is that women have the right to control what occurs in their own bodies. There are techniques of fertilization in which a fetus may grow outside the mother's body. If she should change her mind about having a baby, does she still have the right to determine the fate of the fetus outside her body?

What about surrogate mothers, called gestational carriers, who play no part in producing the fetus they incubate? A woman born without a uterus has her eggs fertilized with her husband's sperm, then the growing fetus is given to another woman. Does that gestational carrier have any say about the other woman's child, which she bears? Could she abort the fetus in her body if she chose to?

Such questions might have merely had the effect of brain teasers rather than encouraging genuine intellectual activity, but at least they would have prodded the extremists toward self-examination. As it was, no one challenged themselves or brought up the many thorny issues inherent in their stances. No one mentioned the history of the subject. Faye Wattleton introduced the value of private deliberation, but only in passing at the end of the forum. And no one really touched upon the personal moral complexities involved, in spite of what Kate Michelman had said in her summary remarks.

In any case, it wasn't genuine compromise that anyone was hearing that night. It was a variety of uncompromising voices, simply sounding more civilized and reasonable than they usually sound in overtly political arenas. Both for what was said and for what was not said that evening, the forum actually showed that it was pretty much impossible to reach an intellectual or ethical compromise on the issue. Learning to live with the irreconcilable was merely hinted at and not explored as a possibility.

What the forum did demonstrate was how mired everyone was—mired in an adamant posture, pro-life or pro-choice, or mired in a kind of quiet resignation. The forum may have been intended to show what a hot and volatile issue abortion is. But in a way the "coldness," the rigidity, of the issue prevailed. Once that evening was over, the nation's television viewers could reasonably feel that if abortion was not absorbed into the normal chaos of American life, along with other difficult problems, it was going to poison the national bloodstream.

Yet an antidote was suggested: When Father McBrien spoke of being religiously and personally opposed to abortion but recognizing that he lived in a country where the majority felt otherwise, he struck a note that seemed to me both authentic and useful. What he was saying indirectly was that personal morality functions in complicated ways in a democracy. Sometimes it coincides with the majority will, sometimes not. Sometimes it cooperates with the way a democracy runs itself. And sometimes it goes against the grain. We live with ourselves, and we live with others. That simple proposition lies at the center of the country's most confounding problems, abortion included.

So many times during the evening the idea had been repeated that compromise on the issue was a possibility. No one said what was meant by the term. Yes, it was easy enough to envisage pro-lifers making concessions on abortion in cases of rape and incest. Easy enough, too, to imagine pro-choice advocates dragging themselves reluctantly toward some variation of parental notification or consent. But neither would such concessions reduce the furor of the polar positions or give the "muddled middle," as Faye Wattleton had called the American majority, a way to live with the issue in a common understanding—to live as one country with one attitude, however complicated, under one set of laws.

The value of *Roe* v. *Wade* when it was established was that it gave the country a single standard under which to operate. The trouble with *Roe* v. *Wade*, as Bork had pointed out, was that people had not had the chance to express themselves on this issue before that single standard was put in place. Bork, in my view, was right when he said that a dismantled *Roe* v. *Wade* would allow the country the opportunity to debate and think for itself at last—though unlike me, Bork seemed to hope that in the end the country would adopt an anti-abortion position. Unlike laws that evolve from commonly agreed upon ideas, *Roe* v. *Wade* was hoisted like a sudden flag over armies still at war. However one felt about the rightness of the Court's decision, there was something wrong about dealing by fiat with an issue so morally complex and personally painful. The best ending to the entire controversy might be the eventual reinstatement of *Roe* v. *Wade* or the legislative equivalent terms of it, but only after people had had the chance to hear what others thought and, more importantly, to discover what they themselves thought.

If the public intellectual debate proved anything, it proved how simpleminded politics made the issue. Even the intellectual debate was political. Yet lay the laws and the elections aside, and abortion remains what it has always been: a personal decision made at a moment of great emotional tension. Abortion is usually the consequence of a mistake, of something gone wrong. The question is how not to compound the wrong. And the matter is made more complicated still by the idea that birth is something good and wonderful and ought to be celebrated, juxtaposed against the sad fact that there are times when it would be the worst of consequences. This confusion of feelings may occur within a social system, but it is still very private business.

Welch and Willke did not see abortion as a private matter. Wattleton and Michelman saw it as a personal choice—that is, a right. But exercising a right is something different from working out a private problem. Many of the panelists were abortion "professionals." They were used to thinking about the issue in public ways—that is, as part of a debate in which there is a clear winner and loser. You could hear their attitudes in their use of language and see it in their faces. Even Gans, who made the most of her personal story, treated it as a public act with public ramifications.

Yet most Americans do not talk about abortion in terms of winning or losing a public debate, even as we concede that the problem has a public identity. As I suggested at the outset, we tend not to talk about it at all, unless someone dear to us is faced with the choice. The point, the value, of the whole country coming to terms with the issue is that it relieves the isolation of someone in that position. It tells her that she is part of a society that has created a place for her predicament. How do we live with one another? How do we live with ourselves?

~~~~

Where we are on abortion, I believe, is not where politics has taken us or where the public debate has taken us but where we are in our private minds. That, unlike the political and intellectual arenas, has been undiscoverable because we do not discuss our thoughts about the subject. Our thoughts are often undisclosed to ourselves, since emotions and impressions move fluidly through the subject with as much authority as ideas and principles.

There is some question as to whether we even want to think about abortion or, for that matter, whether we want to consider any subject of national importance these days. Abortion is but one of several prominent issues—war, poverty, pornography, free speech, homelessness, and race being others—on which there is very little expression of the complexities and ambiguities of private thought. ("I want to help the homeless." "I resent the homeless.") Perhaps such issues are so overwhelming that people forgo thinking about them because they feel powerless to do anything about them. Or perhaps the country is experiencing a period of severe moral laziness in which it is ceding individual responsibility while being content to accept portrayals of national character in the news.

Yet the thinking has to occur anyway, in some insistent if haphazard process that often leaves people dimly aware that they house a number of competing feelings about a subject that seem impossible to organize into a clear definition. When the subject is abortion, I believe most of us may not really wish to reach such a clear definition of feelings, as clarity in one part of our thinking may make another part untrue.

To further complicate matters, there are other issues in the wind that relate to abortion which make our thinking about it both broader and more diffuse:

The issue of individual rights versus the standards of a community has been raised in such various contexts as flag burning and the lyrics of rock songs.

The issue of privacy is at the center of such questions as the debate over mandatory AIDs testing and whether physicians who are HIV-positive ought to inform their patients.

Issues involving men and women and men against women arise in contexts as different as office promotions and acts of violence—gang rape, date rape, sexual harassment, and so forth. The apparent growing hostility of men toward women is, I am fairly certain, at the center of much anti-abortion activity on the part of men. And even those men in favor of abortion rights seem to find other vents for feeling that women are menacing men's place in society. Much of the popularity of the so-called men's movement as prescribed in recent books seems an outgrowth of that threatened feeling—even though the authors of the books condemn such attitudes.

Questions involving the institution of the family impinge on abortion. The decline of the nuclear family, for example, inspires in some people visions of chaos, of children running amok outside traditional structures. The image of the newly liberated woman, who by her freedom inspires traditional pro-family rhetoric, raises the issue as well.

The status of the poor is relevant. The poor worry the rest of society. They have too many children out of wedlock. They require so much federal funding already. Federal funding for abortion would only further drain the economy. No federal funding would (does) result in an increased welfare society.

Scientific experimentation affects thoughts on abortion as well. The menaces or promises of genetic engineering, depending on one's point of view, connect to problems of fate and free will as well as to spiritual matters concerning human limits and divine mysteries.

All such issues touch that of abortion, making it increasingly difficult for most of us to express what it is we think. Yet we also know that the expressions of thought offered by the politicians and the professional debaters do not represent most of us accurately. At bottom, as I said earlier, I believe that most Americans do know what they think about the subject. But we have not yet made that clear to ourselves or to one another.

Where we are privately on abortion is where we are on most of the essential elements of American life—a plane of contradictions. This may turn out not only to be the place where we will be always but also the most appropriate and most useful place to be in a riven society.

Contradiction in American thought is often operative contradiction—that is, a conflicted state of mind in which the country actually functions better than it does when everything is clean and tidy. We are by now used to a certain degree of conflict in all important problems of national life. Very few people who oppose capital punishment do not at one point of their lives think "kill him" when they learn of an especially brutal murderer. People who oppose affirmative action in the workplace often do not oppose it in the context of school admissions, where many different kinds of quotas are quietly filled and acknowledged.

The exceptions may prove the rule in such areas, but as in the feeling that certain killers ought to be put to death, it is by the exceptional circumstances that one knows the entirety of one's true mind. Chances are that the more significant the problem, the less adamant honest thinkers will be considering it. For such honest thinkers there will always be the instructive presence of doubt, which, in a way, provides the individual citizen's balance of power.

The idea of living with conflict does not mean mere

sufferance. Neither individuals nor the country as a whole would be able to succeed by living with conflict if all that meant was grinning and bearing unbearable circumstances. That, I imagine, is the way people in totalitarian states have to learn to gear their thinking. The basic conflict with which people lived in the Soviet Union until recently—everyone employed, everyone suppressed—could not possibly offer a state of mind that was healthy or productive.

But for us living with conflict means an acknowledgment of apparently incompatible elements within an acceptable system—F. Scott Fitzgerald's dictum about one's being able to function while holding contrary thoughts played out on a national stage. We are for both federal assistance and states' autonomy; we are for both the First Amendment and normal standards of propriety; we are for both the rights of privacy and the needs of public health; and so forth. Our most productive thinking usually contains a clear inner confession of mixed feelings, our least productive, a nebulous irritation resulting from a refusal to come to terms with disturbing and patently irreconcilable ideas.

Yet even irreconcilable ideas may be arranged in preferential order. One way to test the proposition that it is preferable for the country to permit abortion than not to permit it is to envisage an America in which abortion is against the law, as it was prior to *Roe*. The terrible helplessness or seething resentment of women forced to give birth because society had decided that this most personal choice belonged to the state and not to the individual would be overwhelming, especially after twenty years during which that state granted individual choice.

Many of us nurture a vision of our country as a place where one can not only make one's own important choices but where one can develop a sense of personal morality by making those choices. That vision would be obscured by any abortion restriction that told a woman the choice was not finally hers. The inner value of presenting choice, real choice, is to offer problems with elements of almost equal merit. Faced with such problems, an individual can grow as much from considering the choice he or she does not make as from the one taken. Conflict of thought is thus not an accident of democracy but a necessary attribute.

I do not believe, by the way, that the introduction of RU-486 in this country, if that should happen, will lessen conflicted thoughts about abortion. The fact that an abortion can be self-administered will only in one sense make the practice easier, in allowing it to be entirely private. But because it will be private, without even a doctor present, the moral burden of the individual woman may be greater. With RU-486 she may make the choice of an abortion without consulting anyone, including a physician or the man involved, and thus may assume a much greater share of the responsibility for the decision than she really wants to have. RU-486 is an abortifacient, not a contraceptive. The only problem it will solve, should abortion ever be legally forbidden and the drug smuggled into the country, would be to create a way around the law, not the mind.

Abortion is too significant a problem to admit adamancy on either side. The problem is distorted when it is considered wholly one way or the other. Not unlike free speech, which is a guaranteed right that admits many misgivings, abortion too should be a guaranteed right that admits misgivings. Those who say that abortion should be avoided as an option by increased sex education and social programs for the poor are expressing misgivings indirectly. But abortion should give pause even when it has proved the only reasonable resort. The act, under any circumstances, involves an interruption of the fundamental process of the species and ought to be troubling always.

That may be why we have had such difficulty in absorbing and facing the complexities of the problem. Abortion is unlike other conflicted national problems. A sense of grief attends it, a grief that discourages open discussion. A great many more families are touched by abortion, experience at least one abortion, than ever talk about it. Those same families will readily discuss divorce in their midst, madness, diseases, even death, but when it comes to abortion they swallow their voices. However sensible it may have been to have an abortion, the decision is usually accompanied by a deep and private sadness. Shame, too, sometimes—shame for taking nature in an unnatural direction, for violating what is perceived as a biological or spiritual law.

It is not women alone who have these feelings. A similar grief is experienced by men, who often feel doubly helpless in the situation. Often it is the man's circumstances that makes abortion the more practical choice. Or the man has persuaded the woman to do something she is unsure of. Or the man wants the child but bows to the woman's decision. Or he simply has participated in an act that has made the decision necessary.

In none of these circumstances is the procedure of the abortion the man's to endure; the immediate pain and depression, if they are felt, are the woman's. The man's peculiar pain and depression come from being very much in the situation and very much out of it simultaneously. He has contributed to a difficulty, but he cannot share its consequences equally. The sorrow he feels is the shadow of sorrow.

These two kinds of grief are not vented in our society. They bury themselves in people's minds and become like an unspoken-of tragedy of the past—never quite gone, never quite forgotten. Not that men and women involved in an abortion decision necessarily regret the act. Some do; some do not. But most experience regret for the necessity of the decision in the first place. For those declared pro-choice as well as those declared pro-life, for most everyone whom the issue touches, abortion is too difficult to speak of, too personal, too mysterious, nobody's business, not even ours.

The resulting silence, I believe, is at the center of the nation's anguish and disruption. The politicians act in the states, the debaters debate on television, but the majority of the country remains troubled and keeps quiet. Consider again the fact that 73 percent of the people support abortion rights and 77 percent think of abortion as a form of murder. What can that mean but that the great majority of the country wants the right to choose an abortion as well as the right to live painfully with its choices?

It also means, in my view, that the majority of the country wants to live painfully with abortion and at the same time to discourage the practice wherever possible. Such discouragement may be effected by things as specific as sex education and the introduction of improved contraceptives such as Norplant and by things as general as increased attention to the poor and to family structure and discipline. In a 1988 study of nineteen Western democracies, only two had a pregnancy rate higher than ours. Only one had a higher abortion rate. Nobody, pro-choice or pro-life, would want to see America move up in those statistics.

The efforts necessary to discourage abortion, however, always seem to be somebody else's job. The scientists have to produce better contraceptives; the schools, better education; religions, higher spirituality; the government, help for the poor. Individuals, choosing to see themselves as living outside these institutions, forfeit responsibility for acting on their own knowledge. Most people not only know how they feel about abortion, they also know how to decrease it. Still, they say nothing.

The danger in this vast silence is that it puts the majority at risk of living in an America that inaccurately represents them on this issue. By opening the question to action by the states, *Webster* effectively gave rise to a disunited country in which the ability to get an abortion depends on where one lives. There are huge practical disadvantages to such a system. A state like Iowa, which

I will look at in the final chapter of this book, in which *Roe* v. *Wade* remains untouched, is nonetheless surrounded by states that have restricted their abortion laws. If the situation remains as it is, women from those surrounding states will pour into Iowa, which then may also restrict its laws to avoid becoming the sole abortion clinic of its region. Abortion is the whole country's problem, and it will only be messed up further than it already has been if each state, an odd political unit in any case, appoints itself as a separate moral authority.

Where we are on abortion is here: Most Americans want to live in a system where people are as responsible as humanly possible for their destinies. Thus, abortion must be preserved as an option. Most of those same Americans also dread the practice of abortion, whether or not they seek other remedies in society that would make abortion less necessary. They simply dislike the practice. In some cases, they abhor it. They approve of a society in which abortion is permitted only because they prefer one evil to another.

This condition of conflict, it seems to me, must be made articulate and explicit. If it is merely inferred without people making their feelings known, without struggling to unearth those feelings themselves, we will have a country made up of either one distortion or the other. Either we will have states acting like independent countries, each with its own moral code, or we will continue to have a national law that sustains the policies of *Roe* but in no way takes cognizance of or encourages citizens who need to express doubts, concerns, or abhorrence. No one will do anything to make abortions less necessary. And pro-life people will always remain at odds with pro-choice people, because neither will bother to make their ambivalence known.

There is another element of thought that each side might make known to the other. Whatever one feels about the role of fate or God in an unsought pregnancy, everyone experiences a unique sense of helplessness when the pregnancy occurs. The feeling of being out of control of one's life, especially in a situation that involves the creation of life, offers a mystery recognizable to anyone, no matter what one's position on abortion per se. The actions taken in response to this mystery will differ, but the feelings of being led or misled by external forces—biological, divine, or both—are universal. People might begin to talk about those feelings as a basis for discussing abortion as well as other confounding elements of modern life.

The whole idea of what choice means is open to such discussions. The more advanced society grows, the more choices people are supposed to have before them. Still, birth and death continue to elude science and technology, as diligently as science and technology try to capture and tame them. Certain people, perhaps most pro-life people, accept those human restraints with pleasure, resignation, or humility. Other people, perhaps most pro-choice people, resist them. Yet that one point of disagreement, which is the focal point of entire philosophies, offers another way into openly discussing the subject of abortion.

And then there is the matter of the consequences of one's choices. Both pro-life and pro-choice advocates make one choice or another regarding an abortion and both must believe that their choice is right. When the choices do not turn out to be right—when the woman who had the baby is burdened beyond endurance or the woman who had the abortion is crippled with remorse—both sides might like to know that there is a source of judgment, in or out of the world, that forgives them and finds their choices, however they might be regretted, as existing within normal fallible human behavior.

Those who choose and those who choose not to choose are equally powerful and equally powerless over their lives. Both might be gratified to know that there is a merciful opinion of their decision somewhere, which in the end may come from one another.

We must be willing to acknowledge and live with an imponderable, agonizing, and fundamentally ambivalent element in our national life, and we have not yet been able to do so. Yet acknowledging and living with ambivalence is, in a way, what America was invented to do. To create a society in which abortion is permitted and its gravity appreciated is to create but another of the many useful frictions of a democracy society. Such a society does not devalue life by allowing abortion; it takes life with utmost seriousness and is, by the depth of its conflicts and by the richness of its difficulties, a reflection of life itself.

Chapter 2
A History of Contradiction

*O*ne look at the history of abortion might make you wonder why America has had such a hard time accepting abortion's contradictions, since the history of the problem is a compendium of contradictory decisions. If Americans were more interested in history generally, we might have examined how various cultures have dealt with this particular problem, noted that no other civilization has come close to solving it, and concluded that the best way was the conflicted way. Instead, we have tended to treat abortion as if it entered human activity with us alone and is our special issue, causing our special anguish. I will address what I think to be the causes of our self-destructive parochialism in Chapter 3. In this chapter, by discussing the history of the subject, I would like to suggest how strange is our avoidance of abortion's conflicted nature, given the contradictory ways everyone else in the world has dealt with it.

The history of abortion is inseparable from other problematical social issues to which abortion is attached. Search the records of ancient civilizations and you will not find a great deal said about abortion per se; the subject will appear as an adjunct to discussions of the status of women, crimes of assault, ownership of property, the rules of medical practice, constructions of ideal societies and population control. Abortion seems to exist in history as an omnipresent problem that becomes controversial from time to time, when the rules of society and the needs of individuals are at odds.

Yet unlike the history of other complicated and nettling ideas, that of abortion does not develop significantly—that is, deepen—over the centuries. The questions that framed the issue four thousand years ago are the same questions framing it today. How these questions are addressed from civilization to civilization depends on such variables as religion, social structure, forms of government, and prevalent philosophies. The questions themselves, however, do not change, probably because in most ways the human condition does not change. Underlying every era and instance in which the issue arises is the same fear and wonder that people are capable of creating and uncreating themselves.

The entire history of the subject expresses itself in three fundamental concerns: 1) When is a fetus a person? 2) What circumstances justify an abortion? 3) Who decides?

The first of these, when addressed by the Greeks, Romans, Jews, and early Christians, involved the existence of the soul. When the soul was said to enter the fetus, a person was formed and abortion was deemed murder. Modern societies have used more scientific standards of personhood, but the problem of calculating the beginnings of life is the same. Abortion has always been tied to speculations as to when beings may be considered human.

The second question, concerning justification, involves the collisions of competing systems of values. Sometimes, historically, the answer to this second question has depended on the answer to the first; it is not permissible to end the existence of a developed or developing person. Other times, the debate over justification concerns population control, as it did in Aristotle's Greece, the Soviet Union of the 1920s, Nazi Germany, or modern China, where abortion is used openly to hold the population down. This question goes directly to the competitive needs of the state and the individual.

The third question—Who decides?—is an extension of the second. Does the choice belong to the individual or to the state? The question also raises the issue of a woman's rights and place in society. Plato, in pursuit of his stark Utopia, advocated forcing certain women to have abortions. Roman law held that all such decisions belonged to the father. Men in medieval and modern societies made the rules governing a woman's freedom—that includes America before *Roe* v. *Wade* and after the *Webster* decision. Since the *Webster* decision, American law has begun to limit a woman's freedom to choose.

All these questions are logically and practically connected, and different societies have chosen to answer them differently. One constant ought to be kept in mind, however, as we move through the history: Every civilization that in one context or another has recorded its attitudes about abortion has taken the issue with the utmost seriousness. Very few societies have given abortion unqualified approval. Most have seen the practice as a violation of nature, whether in the end that violation has been judged necessary, merited, or even good.

I emphasize this point to indicate that to be able to live with abortion does not require us to dismiss its deep seriousness or to regard it merely as a routine convenience of modern life. Life has always been modern to every civilization, yet eternal human verities remain. As long as a human conscience is involved in the decision, abortion will continue to be taken very seriously, as it should be. The value of gaining a sense of the subject's history, I think, is to understand the subject as related to other ambiguous issues that shape a society; that there has never been any universal solution to the problem; and that the individual solutions have only existed within the context of particular societies.

In this chapter I am going to discuss the history of the subject in terms of its three questions, leaving America's own history of abortion for a separate discussion at the chapter's end. The lessons of the general history of abortion suggest that we ought to have been able to make use of the inherent conflicts in the problem and to have added abortion to the other conflicted issues of which our particular society is composed. In fact, for nearly a half century we appeared to take abortion with much more calm and casualness than other countries. And then, over a century and a half, we did not, creating instead a sequence of polar decisions on abortion that led to the present turmoil. The intensity of that turmoil has made us unique in the history of the subject, which is why I wish to take up America separately.

~~~~

Historically, the irresolvable quality of the problem shows up in each of the three basic questions, beginning with When is a fetus a person? The question pertains directly to the sanctity of human life. If human life were not generally considered sacred, no society would have had a problem with abortion; and the extent to which one stage of the developing life was deemed more sacred than another often determined how a particular society dealt with the problem. The essential, pervasive fact is that the concern for human life goes as deep into history as is traceable. That concern forms the foundation of civilized peoples, and pro-choice advocates today, who share that concern, must acknowledge that the pro-life opposition is rooted in it.

Yet the problem of when a fetus becomes a person has not been solved, either. From primitive to modern societies abortion was usually a punishable crime, because human life was considered precious. Whether a fetus represented a human life, however, was only guessed at. What we see in looking at the history of the question of personhood, then, is a contradictory idea itself: Human life is sacred, and no one knows exactly what constitutes human life.

Within four hundred primitive and ancient societies abortion was, and in some cases still is, practiced openly but usually under specific strictures. Punishment for abortions outside those strictures include divorce, beatings, public scorn, fines, exile, and death by drowning. Among some of the Eskimo, a woman who had a premature birth was thought to exude a vapor that drives away seals. The Arapaho American Indians feared that aborted babies would return from the dead to harm or kill their mothers. The Rhade Moi in Indochina believed the ghosts of aborted children would ask the Master of the Universe to send misfortune to the world.

Among such societies there has been no single common answer to the question of when the fetus becomes a person—that is, in the sense of having rights—but the fear that attended abortion clearly had to do with the idea that life was a gift of the gods. Cheyenne Indians have held that an unborn child is a legal person and member of the tribe; abortion is a crime punished by exile. But parents among the natives of Formosa had the right to kill any child who had not yet been named, which happened at age two or three—the naming of the child clearly associated with the definition of a life. Girls who conceived before a certain age aborted. The mother, the father, the tribe, or a part of the tribe made that decision.

The Hindu tradition dating from before 1500 B.C. regarded abortion as the greatest possible sin—an attack on human life. Guilt for abortion could not be expiated. The

Arharva-Veda (written before 1500 B.C.) described how
the gods passed their guilt to a scapegoat, who gave it to
human beings, who gave it by association to Pushan, the
god of wayfarers—sinners who have lost their way in life.
Even he must put the guilt somewhere—"Enter into the
rays, into smoke, O sin; go into the vapours and into the
fog! Lose thyself on the foam of the river! Wipe off, O
Pushan, the misdeeds on him that practiseth abortion!"

Another Hindu book said that a person who eats beef
would be reincarnated as a "strange being" about whom
there is "evil report," such as "he has expelled an embryo
from a woman." Abortion, like eating cattle, was sym-
bolic of ultimate destructiveness, destroying life at its
source. The fetus had a soul, i.e., it contained the eternal
Brahman, "the seed of all beings." A later book, the
Anugita, described how the "soul, entering the limbs of
the fetus, part by part . . . supports [them] with the mind.
Then the fetus, becoming possessed of consciousness,
moves about its limbs. As liquefied iron being poured out
assumes the form of the image, such you must know is
the entrance of the soul into the fetus . . ."

This is one of the earliest references to the soul as a
sign of humanity. The process of "ensoulment" was later
translated as "quickening" and then "viability."

Legal codes before the Greeks sought to protect pregnant women from violence in order to protect the fetus.
Under the Sumerian Code (c. 2000 B.C.), anyone who
struck a pregnant woman and induced a miscarriage
risked a fine. A deliberate blow incurred a greater fine
than an accidental one. The Code of Hammurabi (c. 1800
B.C.) similarly fined a man who killed a fetus by striking

a pregnant woman, with the severity of the fine depending on the mother's condition. If she died and was of the highest social rank, the guilty man's daughter was executed—women seemed to lose out either way. "If a seignior struck a[nother] seignior's daughter and caused her to drop that of her womb, he shall pay 10 shekels of silver for her fetus. If that woman has died, they shall put his daughter to death." Causing a commoner's daughter to miscarry incurred a fine of 5 shekels; her death cost a half mina of silver. A female slave's miscarriage cost 2 shekels and the death a third mina of silver. Neither code mentioned the age of the fetus. But the precision of the fines would indicate that life was given various concrete values.

The Assyrians seem to be the first people on record whose law answered the question of when human life begins. They regarded the fetus as a human life and discussed the stages of its development. The Assyrian Code (c. 1500 B.C.) demanded severe penalties, including death, for a man who struck another man's pregnant wife and killed her fetus. And if a woman deliberately aborted her own child, she would be impaled without burial. The code followed a "life for a life" principle, on the idea that the life of the fetus was the father's property.

The emphasis on the father's loss may be seen in the details of the code: The striker was put to death if the woman died or if her husband did not have a son (even if the fetus was a girl). If the woman survived and her husband did have a son, the striker still had to "compensate for her fetus with a life"—i.e., not his own, but some life considered his to dispose of. The rationale for such laws would seem to suggest that the central issue was property. Yet the property in question had such great value that its loss was a justification for severe punishment.

Similarly, the Hittite Code (c. 1300 B.C.) prescribed fines for abortion depending upon whether the woman was in the fifth or ninth month of pregnancy, implying a calculus of increasing life or value. "If anyone causes a free woman to miscarry, if [it is] the tenth month, he shall give 10 shekels of silver. If [it is] the fifth month, he shall give five shekels and pledge his estate as security." Germain Grisez, author of *Abortion: the Myth, the Realities, and the Arguments,* speculates that the fine increased a shekel each month. Fines also varied according to the status of the woman: The miscarriage of a slave cost 5 shekels in the ninth month and nothing in the fifth month. A later version of the Hittite laws dropped the references to months and increased the fines. In the late version: "If anyone causes a free woman to miscarry, he shall give 20 shekels of silver and 10 shekels for the miscarriage of a slave woman."

Zoroastrians believed that life came from the good principle, and death from evil. Killing was a concession to the evil principle. Zoroastrianism may have influenced Western thought as a reform of traditional Persian beliefs at the time of the Jewish exile from Palestine.

Later, Hindu legal codes (500 B.C. and after) seemed to indicate that the fetus was not as sacred as it had been earlier. The code condemned abortion but not with the horror of the *Arharva-Veda.* Abortion became a lesser and lesser crime, and then only if the embryo destroyed was of unknown sex and therefore possibly male. From being the ultimate sin, abortion became a sin against the husband equal to wasting his property.

An early compilation of laws ranks abortion with the murder of a husband or a learned Brahman; the act made a woman an outcast. Another treats it merely as a reason for divorce; another ranks it a less serious crime than stealing gold from a Brahman, drinking liquor, or committing adultery, and it is listed at all only if the embryo could have been male. A later Hindu code (c. the birth of Christ) ranks it as a sign of impurity, requiring penance only if the embryo was possibly male. The code Narada, compiled several hundred years after Christ, holds that a wife who wastes her husband's property, makes an attempt on her life, or induces abortion is to be banished from the town.

By the time we get to the Greeks, it is clear that abortion is treated with a variety of conflicting attitudes, even within a single culture. The scholarly literature disagrees about whether ancient Greece legislated against abortion. It is known that abortions were commonplace, and "exposing" infants even more so. Exposed infants—that is, infants cast out and left to die in the elements—were killed by animals or captured and sold into slavery or prostitution.

The idea of the existence of a soul as a sign of human life was picked up by the later Greeks. Pythagoras (c. 580–497 B.C.) believed in transmigration of souls; a soul moved from one body to the next seeking purification so that it could ultimately return to heaven. Pythagoreans are reported by ancient sources to have argued that the soul entered the fetus at conception—an implicit argument against abortion for any purpose, even to save the mother's life, according to one philosopher, Paul Carrick *(Medical Ethics in Antiquity)*. The ensoulment debate begun with the Hindus would carry through to the Christians.

Plato's successors at the Academy held that the soul entered the body not in utero but through the infant's first breath. This position provides moral grounds for permitting broad use of abortion. Plato himself had Socrates prescribe in the Republic (V, 459) that all children conceived outside the bounds of his eugenic program be aborted or killed at birth.

Aristotle (384–322 B.C.), in his *Politics*, argued that abortion should be lawful only before the fetus has acquired "sense and life." In a different text, his *History of Animals*, he speculated that a male embryo acquires distinct parts or form around the fortieth day and a female embryo acquires form about the ninetieth day. (The language about form would be taken up in the Christian distinction between the "formed" and the "unformed" fetus.) Aristotle's followers concluded that forty and ninety days were his cut-off points for abortion, although it would have been impossible for a mother in antiquity to adhere to them accurately. She could not have known the sex of an unborn child; even assuming the fetus was male, she would not have known the precise day of conception. (A woman on a twenty-eight-day cycle would have missed only one period.)

Aristotle himself outlined a progression in utero from a nutritive soul (which was what he meant by "life" in *Politics*), to a sensitive soul (what he meant by "sense"), and then to a rational soul, but he does not give timelines. Like Plato, he prescribed a eugenic program regulating marriage and sex, and called for laws limiting family size. Once a family had had the required number of children, abortions would be compulsory. Again like Plato, he implicitly denied abortion except where required by the state; in his view, the only public purpose for abortion was to control overpopulation. In other words, he placed the sanctity of life below the state's welfare, yet he was much concerned with the question of when life begins. Since Aristotle also limited abortions to the time before the fetus has "sense" (whenever that may be), he was much more restrictive of abortions than Plato.

Another indication of Greek thought on the subject is the Oath of Hippocrates (460–357 B.C.), which forbade doctors to assist in abortions by administering pessaries, a poison introduced directly into the womb through the birth canal. But Hippocrates was said to have thought other means acceptable. The Romans would pick up on this distaste for poisons in the Lex Cornelia.

Greek religion did not demonstrate any special concern for the unborn, although Greek inscriptions on temples describe birth, miscarriage, and abortion as occasions of ritual impurity. A woman was to abstain from worship and follow purification rituals after any of these events.

Very much concerned with the sanctity of human life, Jews in Alexandria and Palestine, along with the rest of the ancient world, debated the issue of ensoulment. In the Talmud, the rabbinic law based on the Torah compiled about A.D. 500, opinions were presented as to whether ensoulment occurs at conception, during the first trimester, at birth, or as one rabbi had it, when the child first answered "Amen." The Talmud concluded that the question was unanswerable and irrelevant to abortion.

Elsewhere the Talmud held that the fetus was part of the mother. The Mishnah, an earlier rabbinic code that became the basis for the Talmud, commanded that a fetus be destroyed if necessary to save a woman whose life was endangered during labor. But once the head or the greater part of the fetus had emerged from her body, it could not be touched because "we may not set aside one life for another."

The fetus thus acquires the status of a newborn, or "life," when it is half born. The scriptural basis of this teaching was Exodus 21:22–25, which echoes the Sumerian code and the Code of Hammurabi. According to Exodus, if two men were fighting and one struck a pregnant woman so hard she miscarried, he would be ordered to pay a fine compensation to the woman's husband. Should the mother die, the "eye for an eye" rule applied and the man would be executed.

The rabbis commenting on Exodus in the Mishnah concluded that if abortion could be punished merely by a fine, it could not be murder.

A separate Jewish tradition arose from the same passage in Exodus in the Septuagint, the Greek translation of the Old Testament produced between 300–200 B.C. (The Talmud is based on the Hebrew translation.) In the Septuagint, the Hebrew word *ason*, or "harm," was rendered as "form," introducing the Aristotelian view of the beginnings of life. As a result, the text now required the striker to pay a fine compensating the woman's husband if the fetus was not yet fully formed. If the fetus was formed, the man would be put to death. If killing a formed fetus (as opposed to killing a pregnant woman) was a capital crime, then abortion after a certain point in fetal development was murder.

The Samaritans and Karaites and the Jewish philosopher Philo of Alexandria (25 B.C.–A.D. 41) all considered abortion a capital crime, which means that the life taken was judged to be human thus sacred. Philo compared the fetus to a statue in an artist's studio that needed only to be carried outside to realize life: "If a man comes to blows with a pregnant woman and strikes her on the belly and she miscarries, then, if the result of the miscarriage is unshaped and undeveloped, he must be fined both for the assault and for obstructing the artist Nature in her creative work of bringing into life the fairest of living creatures, man. But, if the offspring is already shaped and all the limbs have their proper qualities and places in the system, he must die, for that which answers to this description is a human being, which he has destroyed in the laboratory of Nature who judges that the hour has not yet come for bringing it out into the light, like a statue lying in a studio requiring nothing more than to be conveyed outside and released from confinement." Other Jewish Alexandrian writings warn the Jews against the pagan practice of general abortion.

The fact that the Talmudic law considered the fetus part of the mother has been cited in modern pro-choice arguments. Talmudic law did, however, make abortion mandatory during a life-threatening labor. The mother and father had no choice; the mother could not choose suicide and the father could not sacrifice her life. Abortion for any other reason was not even discussed in rabbinic laws; scholars agree that this was because the practice was virtually unknown among Jews, who followed the command to be fruitful and multiply.

Among the Romans, the answer to When is a fetus a person? was simple: The fetus became human at birth. The Roman Stoic Seneca held to the general Stoic view, based on Plato, that human life began with the first breath. Until birth, the fetus was merely part of the mother's body, analogous to the fruit of a tree. Until the fruit ripened, she could do with it as she wished. Roman law and custom, however, required the father's consent.

The Stoics further believed that only "rational" beings, those fourteen years or older, had political rights such as protection from homicide. While Seneca and the Stoic Musonius Rufus argued against abortion on the grounds that bearing children was a religious and civic virtue, they spoke in contradiction to the general Roman callous attitudes toward human life evidenced by gladiators, crucifixions, and infanticide; in Rome abortion was widespread.

The decision to keep or to kill a fetus or newborn fell under the authority of the paterfamilias, or patriarch, who governed the family life of free women. As late as 200 B.C., only he could punish a free woman even for the crime of murdering her husband. Abortions were a matter of personal convenience, depending upon the decision of the paterfamilias. Publicly admitted reasons for abortion included a freeborn woman's desire to preserve her sexual attractiveness or to avoid the burden of caring for the young.

Abortion was a crime only if it was enacted against the father's will. The earliest reference in Roman law to abortion dated from the Monarchy (753–c. 510 B.C.), when a husband was legally permitted to divorce his wife if she aborted his child. No laws against abortion per se existed during the Republic (c. 510–27 B.C.) or the early Empire (27 B.C.–305 A.D.).

In the Lex Cornelia (c. 81 B.C.), laws against assassins and poisoners could be enforced against those who sold abortifacients; if the mother died, the seller was executed. Otherwise the guilty poor were condemned to the mines, while the noble were exiled to an island. There is some scholarly disagreement about whether this law was directed at abortion or if it was enforced.

Cicero (c. 65 B.C.) reported the execution of a Milesian woman who had an abortion, but her specific offense was accepting a bribe from relatives to abort without her husband's consent.

Septimus Severus (193–211 A.D.), a reform emperor, decreed exile for the wife who deliberately deprived her husband of children. Another imperial decree punished a wife who aborted the fetus of her divorced husband. It is argued that Septimus Severus was influenced by the spread of Christianity, which declared from the beginning that abortion was murder. With Christianity, as with early Judaism, we in a sense enter the modern era of thought on the subject, in that the fetus is considered a life and the different attitudes on abortion depend on what stages of development the life achieves.

The earliest Christian documents referring to abortion were *The Didache* [or teaching] *of the Apostles* and the *Epistle of Barnabas*, both affirming the sanctity of life and dating from the early second century and drawing on sources in the late first century. Both contained sections based on a Jewish tradition known as the "Two Ways"— the way of life and the way of death, or the way of light and the way of darkness. Abortion was forbidden as part of the way of death and was included in lists of "thou shalt not" statements detailing proper moral conduct. While *The Didache* presented abortion as a violation of the second commandment ("Love thy neighbor as thyself"), the authors of the Epistle of Barnabas preceded their abortion prohibition with the command "Thou shalt love thy neighbor more than thy own life." Michael J. Gormon (*Abortion and the Early Church*) concludes: "The fetus is seen not as a part of its mother, but as a neighbor. Abortion is rejected as contrary to other-centered neighbor love." It was also explicitly called murder. These teachings could suggest that no one should have the authority to choose an abortion and no purposes justify one.

The *Apocalypse of Peter*, the most important of the noncanonical works, appeared at the same time or just after *The Didache* and *Epistle*. It described a hell in which "the discharge and excrement of the tortured ran down and became like a lake. And there sat women, and the discharge came up to their throats; and opposite them sat many children, who were born prematurely, weeping. And from them went forth rays of fire and smote the women on the eyes. And these were those who produced children outside marriage and who procured abortions."

Another version of this apocalypse provided for the salvation of the infants: "And the children shall be given to the [caretaking, protecting] angel Temlakos. And those who slew them will be tortured for ever, for God wills it to be so." Here the unborn is seen as a living being destined for eternity.

In the same period, Tertullian (c. 160–c.240) defended Christianity against accusations of treason in his Apology, directed at the Roman provincial governors and the emperor Septimus Severus. In his defense against a rumor that the Christians practiced a rite in which they killed a child and ate it (perhaps based on a misunderstanding of the Eucharist), Tertullian said that on the contrary, Christians slaughtered neither the born nor unborn child. "To hinder a birth is merely a speedier man-killing; nor does it matter whether you take away a life that is born, or destroy one that is coming to the birth. That is a man which is going to be one; you have the fruit already in the seed."

Although dependent on the mother, the fetus was not considered a mere part of her. Abortion could still be classified as murder. "In our case, murder being once for all forbidden, we may not destroy even the fetus in the womb, while as yet the human being derives blood from other parts of the body for its sustenance."

In *De anima* (*On the Soul*), Tertullian made an interesting appeal to mothers to decide on the status of the fetus: "In this matter, the best teacher, judge, and witness is the sex that is concerned with birth. I call on you, mothers, whether you are now pregnant or have already borne children; let women who are barren and men keep silence! We are looking for the truth about the nature of woman; we are examining the reality of your pains. Tell us: Do you feel any stirring of life within you in the fetus? Does your groin tremble, your sides shake . . . are not these moments a source of joy and assurance that the child within you is alive and playful?"

His argument prefigures the logic underlying the modern pro-choice position, yet Tertullian clearly assumed that mothers would agree with his anti-abortion stance.

By the tenth century, however, when local councilor legislation was standardized into a churchwide canon, abortion was considered homicide by the Church only if the fetus was formed; otherwise it was a serious sin but not a homicide, because the unformed fetus was not a person. The debate over "form," and later "animation," which echoes the Aristotelian stages and the first ideas of ensoulment, was taken up by the early Church fathers and answered variously in local councils in England and Ireland and the continent.

The early Church fathers either did not mention the distinction between a "formed" and an "unformed" fetus or mentioned it as irrelevant. Others considered it a sound basis for law but stressed that abortion was nonetheless a sin even if not classified as homicide. St. Basil the Great of Caesarea (c. 330–379), one of the esteemed Eastern Church fathers, called abortion murder, affirmed the ten-year penance, and specifically stated when asked that there was no need to distinguish between a formed and an unformed fetus.

St. Augustine (354–430), commenting on the Septuagint version of Exodus, argued that only abortion of the formed fetus was murder, although any abortion was a damnable sin. He considered that the fetus became formed at about six and a half weeks of pregnancy, but he declared that the question of when the soul entered a fetus was unanswerable.

Local councilor law diverged depending upon location; while in Britain and Ireland reduced penances for very early abortion were standard, no distinctions based on fetal age were made in Burgundy, Spain, and Cambria, where churches adhered to the ten-year penance.

In France, abortion of the "animated" fetus was considered murder until the revolution and punished accordingly. As late as the first Bourbon period (1589–1793), doctors and midwives who assisted abortions were sentenced to hanging.

A French law of 1791 reduced the penalty to twenty years in prison. The Napoleonic Code of 1810 set the term of punishment as an indefinite "limited time," without mentioning animation or fetal age. In 1787, Austria under Joseph II dropped its death penalty for abortion.

The earliest collections of English law defined abortion as homicide. An administrator of the king's law in the mid-thirteenth century wrote that someone "who has struck a pregnant woman, or has given her poison, whereby he has caused abortion, if the fetus be already formed or animated, and particularly if it be animated, he commits homicide." Grisez notes that the king's law, like the Church penitentials, were confused as to whether to use the formed or animated distinction. He speculated that "formed" probably meant a recognizably human embryo, while "animated" may have meant one that showed signs of life after delivery.

One would assume a strong Protestant influence on the treatment of abortion in British and American law. But the Reformation did not add substantially to views on the issue. Martin Luther and John Calvin said very little about abortion, and when Protestant authors did speak of it, they tended to repeat the Catholic teachings. In British common law, abortion gradually entered a category referred to as misprision—less than a capital crime but close to one. (Sir Edward Coke, 1552–1634, first used the term *misprision* for abortion.) Life was held to begin not at "formation" or "animation" but at "quickening," when the fetus first moves in the womb, usually at the end of the fourth or beginning of the fifth month.

The British began to speak of a "right" to life after quickening. In the words of the eighteenth-century scholar William Blackstone, "life is the immediate gift of God, a right inherent by nature in every individual; and it begins in the contemplation of law as soon as an infant is able to stir in the mother's womb." Blackstone offers a good summary of the British common-law position before the nineteenth century. He goes on to refer to the ancient concerns with poisons (as in the Lex Cornelia) and a woman struck (as in Exodus): "If a woman is quick with child, and by a potion, or otherwise, killeth it in her womb; or if anyone beat her, whereby the child dieth in her body, and she is delivered of a dead child; this, though not murder, was by the ancient law homicide or manslaughter." Blackstone then explains, "At present it is looked upon in not quite so atrocious a light, though it remains a very heinous misdemeanor. An infant in the mother's womb is supposed in law to be born for many purposes." He had in mind inheritance and guardianship.

Beyond the quickening distinction, there was nothing in the law as to which purposes justified an abortion or who should decide. A London medical convocation in 1756 announced that abortions to save a woman's life were acceptable.

Abortion before quickening did not become a British crime until 1803, when abortion got caught up in the British debate between those who wanted to reduce the severity of the law in general and those who sought to maintain it. In 1803, Parliament passed an omnibus crime statute called Lord Ellenborough's Act. Lord Ellenborough, a conservative chief justice who was upset at the number of crimes that were no longer capital offenses, created as many capital felonies as he could imagine in his omnibus bill. Thus the first British statute to mention abortion departed radically from the common-law tradition. Abortion before quickening was now punishable by whipping, pillory, imprisonment, or exile to a penal colony for up to fourteen years; after quickening, it was punishable by death.

From the nineteenth century to the present, the question of when a fetus is a person did not change as it affected abortion laws in modern society, nor did it come any closer to being answered. When I come to the history of abortion in America, we will see that the personhood of a fetus has never been satisfactorily answered here, either; for all the standards applied in various societies, no one has ever been able to prove when a person comes into being. As I said in Chapter 1, I do not base my feeling that we ought to be able to live with abortion's contradictions on whether or not the fetus is a person; I am ready to concede that a fetus is some form of person. I simply believe that our social priorities require that abortion be permitted. Still, it is important to note that this question of personhood is not now, nor has it ever been, settled. In a way, the fetus itself is an entity of uncertainty and as such reflects the ambiguities as well as the sanctity of the life it represents.

The question What circumstances justify an abortion? has been answered historically with no greater confidence or universality than the personhood question and has depended entirely on the social context in which it has been raised. Rape, incest, illegitimacy, protecting the woman's life, or preserving the milk for children already born are among the sanctioned reasons for abortion. The Aztecs considered abortion a capital crime except if the woman's life was at risk. Ancient Korean law legalized the termination of a pregnancy caused by rape.

As noted before, among the early Hindus, the Assyrians, the Hittites, and early Jews, nothing but the endangerment of the mother's life justified an abortion. With the Greeks entered the idea that abortion was justifiable as a means of regulating the size and nature of a population.

We can tell what circumstances did or did not justify abortions by the punitive reactions of different societies. The first Christian body to enact punishment for abortion was the Council of Elvira (305), a meeting of nineteen bishops from across Spain. They decreed that a woman who aborted a child conceived in adultery would be kept from communion until death.

The Council of Ancyra (314), legislating for churches across Asia Minor and Syria, softened the punishment to various degrees of penance for ten years, in contrast to willful murder, which carried a penalty of penance for life. The ten-year penance became standard into the Middle Ages and was often interpreted as applying to the mere attempt to abort, even if unsuccessful. The councils did not distinguish between stages of fetal development, and neither mentioned the father or the abortionist.

The nonjustifiability of abortion continued into the Middle Ages. When Gratian standardized the various councilor laws into a canon for the entire Church (c. 1140), he excluded accidental abortion and abortion of the nonanimated or nonformed fetus from the category of murder. Pope Gregory IX, in his decretals (1234), which had the force of law for the entire Church, included a letter (1211) by Pope Innocent III that distinguished the "vivified" from the "non-vivified" fetus. Interpreters of this canon adopted the Aristotelian formula of forty days for the male embryo and ninety for the female.

In Spain and France, civil law followed councilor law

in forbidding abortion. As early as the sixth century, the law of the Visigoths in Spain sentenced to death anyone who gave a drug to cause abortion. Slavewomen who aborted were beaten; gentlewomen were degraded. The Chindasvinto Visigoth law in the seventh century punished both the abortionist and a husband who ordered or permitted an abortion; they could be executed or blinded.

After the Middle Ages, abortion, however widespread the practice, was still considered a generally unacceptable act with few justifiable circumstances, and continued as such into the modern era.

In Britain the penalties for early abortion had stiffened as early as 1837. An 1837 amendment to Lord Ellenborough's Act represented a compromise between those who wanted to reduce the number of capital offenses and those who wanted tougher penalties for early abortion. It removed the reference to quickening and eliminated the death penalty, simply stating that abortion at any stage was punishable by not less than fifteen years' to life imprisonment.

By 1861, Parliament had made any attempt to abort, by the woman herself or others, a felony punishable by penal servitude up to life or prison. This law, which would be inherited throughout the commonwealth, remained virtually the same until 1967. Judicial interpretation created a precedent for therapeutic abortion.

The situation was much the same across Europe. Abortion was generally forbidden and considered unjustifiable, while it also grew increasingly common. In Catholic Belgium and France, anti-abortion statutes made no exceptions for therapeutic abortions as late as 1939; the laws, however, remained unenforced. In Lutheran Denmark, Norway, Sweden, and Iceland, the laws in effect until the 1930s again made no explicit exceptions, but official policy permitted abortion to protect the woman's life and health. In Germany, judges interpreted a restrictive law to permit therapeutic abortion.

One opening in the general wall of official condemnation of abortion came from the communist and radical political movements. In Russia, abortion had been forbidden before the revolution under all circumstances. Then, on November 18, 1920, the new Soviet Commissariats of Health and Justice announced that abortions would be available to all who sought them, without charge, in Soviet hospitals. Only physicians in those hospitals could induce abortion. Others, and physicians inducing abortion in private practice, were subject to trial by a people's court.

The Soviet experiment in free, legal abortion inspired movements to liberalize abortion law throughout the West. Argentina's Radical party passed a law in 1921 that explicitly permitted abortion to protect the woman's life or health or if the pregnancy resulted from rape or if the mother was insane or mentally impaired. The World League for Sexual Reform met for the first time in Berlin in 1921. Its 1929 International Congress in London heralded the Soviet example and voted for the "abolition of penalties for the mother and a revision of laws relating to abortion so as to make possible for a woman to obtain a termination of pregnancy on economic, social, and eugenic grounds. . . ." The league's members then included

Sigmund Freud, Havelock Ellis, and Margaret Sanger. That same year, Parliament went so far as to explicitly permit abortions to save a woman's life, but the murkily written statute raised more questions than it answered.

One of the bitterest battles over abortion liberalization was fought in Germany between 1920 and 1933, when the Nazis passed a compulsory sterilization act called the Law for the Prevention of Hereditary Diseases in Posterity. Under the Nazi statute, a pregnant woman selected for sterilization might also be forced to undergo an abortion if the fetus was not already viable. A physician might induce abortion to avert serious danger to a woman's life or health. Except in emergencies, such operations had to be approved by a panel of doctors.

The Nazi law was the first to use the viability of the fetus as a dividing line. Grisez, who opposes abortion, sees in the Nazi abortion law and the events that followed a common link in disrespect for human life. He writes "the leading members of the medical profession were quite prepared by 1933 to put into effect the Nazi program of selective sterilization and abortion, and this same medical profession itself organized and pushed ahead the euthanasia program of the late 1930's which merged into the genocide program of 1941–1945."

In 1935, Iceland legislated that abortion might be justifiably induced during the first eight weeks of pregnancy to protect a woman's life or health. But eight weeks was not held to be an inviolable point when life began. In cases of grave danger to the mother, abortion could be induced later. Again, the doctor decided: Two physicians in every case were required to submit to the country's chief medical officer a signed statement of the reasons for the abortion.

The Icelandic law represented a compromise between those for whom only medical purposes justified abortion and those who wanted doctors to have greater leeway. There were many justifiable purposes for an abortion, according to this law, and each was delineated. In judging probable danger to the woman's health, doctors were instructed to consider "whether the woman has already borne many children at short intervals and a short time has passed since her last confinement, also whether her domestic conditions are difficult, either on account of a large flock of children, poverty, or serious ill health of other members of the family." Three years later, the law was broadened to permit abortion in cases of pregnancy by rape and to prevent the birth of children likely to inherit defects.

A Danish law in 1937 similarly relied on an expanded definition of health. Chronic malnutrition, exhaustion from many pregnancies, and suicide attempts were all official grounds for abortion. Abortions were to be induced only in the first three months, except in cases of a strict "medical" indication.

The year before, the Soviet Union had backtracked to place limits on abortion. After an upsurge in abortion and the decimation of the rural population during the late 1920s due to famine, on June 27, 1936, a new decree forbade abortion unless the pregnancy threatened the life or health of the woman or when a serious disease of the parents could be inherited. The new decree declared that legalizing abortion had been necessary while the last vestiges of exploitation and its consequences were being overcome. But it was now necessary in the interest of both the Soviet woman's "emancipation" and her "great and responsible duty of giving birth to and bringing up citizens" to "combat a light-minded attitude toward family and family obligations." In other words, the welfare of the state was justification enough. Grisez argues that the new decree was "a measure to step-up population growth in order to make up for war losses and to provide the population input needed for postwar expansion."

In 1938, a British judge affirmed that doctors have a duty to perform abortions to safeguard a woman's mental health when he acquitted an obstetrician named Alex Bourne, who had induced abortion in a fourteen-year-old victim who had been raped by two soldiers. The "purpose of preserving the life of the mother shall be construed" in "a reasonable sense," wrote the judge, to apply to situations where in the doctor's opinion, continuance of the pregnancy would "make the woman a physical or mental wreck." Despite this precedent, the availability of abortion in Britain continued to vary greatly.

In 1948 Japan passed its Eugenic Protection Law, setting aside the prohibition of abortion it had passed some fifty years earlier. The 1948 statute as amended in 1952 permitted designated physicians to perform an abortion whenever they believed the mother's health would be hurt by bearing a child. Economic hardship was officially declared a health consideration, in effect making abortions available on request. In *Abortion: The Clash of Absolutes*, Laurence H. Tribe writes that fear of the pill has since made abortion in Japan "a—if not the—primary means of birth control" and that "the medical profession has worked to prevent the introduction of other means . . . in order to prevent competition with its extremely profitable abortion business."

Religious belief is not an important obstacle to abortion in Japan, though Japanese Buddhists hold memorial services for the souls of aborted fetuses and erect monuments at temples to *mizuko* (an aborted fetus, directly translated as "water child" or "unseeing child"). They believe that a *mizuko*'s soul returns to a children's limbo, waiting to be reborn into the same family that aborted it. Shinto believers may make offerings to an aborted fetus to dissuade it from avenging itself on the woman.

Japanese justify abortion for medical or economic reasons, seldom mentioning the woman's right to choose.

In 1953, postrevolutionary China loosened its abortion restrictions, which had been established when the Western powers made "modernization" a condition for withdrawal. (It is interesting that restrictions on abortion were considered "modern.") Since then, abortion policy has depended on state population goals. The current one-child-per-family law involves both financial incentives and compulsory abortions.

In 1955, the Soviet prohibition of abortion was repealed. The prologue of this decree offered three reasons: Social and economic progress had advanced to the stage that measures to encourage motherhood and education would suffice to make the prohibition unnecessary; legalizing abortion would limit the harm done to women by abortions outside hospitals; and finally, legalizing abortion would give "women the possibility of deciding by themselves the question of motherhood."

None of the Soviet decrees addressed directly or indirectly the question of when life began. By 1955, the purpose justifying an abortion seemed to be whatever a woman chose; a survey found that lack of housing, inadequate care facilities, and too many or too close births were the chief reasons given by a sample of twenty-six thousand women having abortions after legalization; about one third, however, simply did not want to have a baby. The decision was legally a woman's. Yet the Soviet laws seem to have been motivated by the state's population needs, as they would have been in Aristotle's ideal society. Most of the Eastern Bloc decriminalized abortion in the post-Stalin period, but in several countries, women have been required to obtain official permission from the local committees. Tribe concludes that in China, the Eastern Bloc, the former Soviet Union, and India, abortion policy remains a matter of population control.

In 1964, the Islamic grand mufti of Jordan approved abortions of an "unformed" fetus, setting the cut-off point at twenty days. The majority of Muslims today seem to believe in abortion before "ensoulment," set at forty to 120 days, depending on national traditions. A minority of scholars argue that all contraception, including abortion, is infanticide. The conservative Muslims are especially influential in India and dominant in Pakistan. This alone suggests the range of opinion on the question of justification today.

What stands out in this survey is that abortion was

justifiable to a society only as it reflected that society's composition and character. The Greek or Roman utopian visions were starkly different from the Jewish or Christian ideals. And within the modern Judeo-Christian tradition, standards of justification have also differed according to a particular society's degree of democracy. Nazi eugenics or Catholic edicts, however different in purpose, both emanated from authoritarian postures. The Soviet Union excepted, societies in which there has been less central control have seen more justifications for abortion.

But the point here, as with the question of personhood, is that the justifiability of abortion has never been universally determined. Between the extremes of convenience and total impermissibility existed a myriad of responses, all of which were fitted to the particular structure of a particular people.

~~~~

The history of the third question, Who decides? is as brief and simple as its answer: Men. Whether we are looking at the elders of an Eskimo tribe, the Roman senate, or the Church fathers, men have always decided the fate of women on this matter. Nor did things change in America, as a look at our history will show. The Supreme Court is composed almost entirely of men, as are the U.S. Congress and the state legislatures. Whatever happens to abortion in this country, men will make it happen, even though they may not suffer the anguish or the consequences that attend the act.

Historically, there were exceptions to male control of the issue. In Futuna, near Fiji, a girl abided by the decision of the women of her neighborhood. Old Germanic tribal law did not penalize the woman who aborted, as it was her right to do so. Anyone who helped her, however, was punished by the group. The Jivaro of Ecuador believed that a woman who bathed in a river might be impregnated by a demon and conceive a monster. She had the right to abort a monster child. Grisez states that the belief was a cover to allow women to abort at will.

And the historical male dominance of the issue does not mean that men were always exempt from responsibility. As we have seen, men under the Hittite code and early Jewish law were held culpable for pain inflicted on pregnant women. The *Vendidad* (c. 600 B.C.), one of the sacred books of Zoroastrianism in what is now eastern Iran, had a positive program to replace abortion. Fathers were charged with supporting a woman during her pregnancy. In fact, if a father failed to do so and a mother died, he would pay the penalty for "willful murder."

Still, these were rules to cover acceptable conduct in society. The specific decision as to what justified an abortion was left to men.

While the male and female aspect of the issue never changed, however, the ambiguity of Who decides? became ambiguous in another context. As societies progressed and democratic forms increasingly became the way of the world, the question of who decides became a continuing contest between individual rights and state or community rights. In the modern world and in America particularly, individuals—women as well as men—are supposed to have a considerable degree of control over their futures. Yet again and again their desire for control collides with community attitudes which, if they do not always oppose individual rights, make them less absolute.

In abortion, as in many other matters, we cannot move along one line of thought without soon being intercepted by another; the community intersects the individual; the individual, the community. Authoritarian societies would not permit that conflict to arise in the open, since individuality threatened state power. Democratic societies, however, try to balance the conflict, which makes America's own history with abortion extremely odd.

~~~~

As I trace our history with respect to the subject, you will see that when the country began we appeared to be perfectly content to live with lenient abortion laws and to look the other way when the existing laws were broken. Yet for reasons described below, we changed into a society that swung dramatically one way and then the other in terms of laws. What changed more gradually was our national anxiety about abortion as a moral issue. Slowly, over time, it grew clear that abortion in America was causing much greater emotional upheaval than it seemed to do in any other society, contemporary or in the past. In Chapter 3, as noted earlier, we will discuss why a country that should have been able to live with the practice of abortion as one of its characteristic conflicts has not. For now, I would like to show how we evolved— somewhat haphazardly—from apparent placidity or tolerance to the turbulence that has made us an historical anomaly.

In the same year, 1803, that Britain adopted Lord

Ellenborough's Act, stiffening the punishment for abortion, an American physician named Thomas Percival wrote in a standard text of medical ethics that abortion should be induced only if the pelvis was "such as to render the birth of a full grown child impossible or inevitably fatal." His book would remain standard reading among a certain class of physicians throughout the century and would eventually have great effect. At the time of publication, however, America was content to apply the quickening distinction long after it was rejected by Percival.

A decade later, in 1812, the Massachusetts Supreme Court ignored the new British harshness against early abortion in a decision that would become the ruling common law precedent through 1850. The court dismissed charges against the unfortunately named Isaiah Bangs because the woman to whom he had given an abortifacient was not "quick" with child.

Throughout the early nineteenth century, American law continued to be more lenient than the British. The first state statutes, in Connecticut (1821), Missouri (1825), and Illinois (1827), punished abortion only after quickening and only when poisons were used. The historian James C. Mohr (*The Historical Character of Abortion in the United States*) describes them as "poison control statutes" (similar to the Lex Cornelia in ancient Rome), designed to protect women from deadly poisons. Iowa passed its poison control statute in 1839. Later, other states with such statutes added instrumental abortion as an offense, again after quickening.

The first attack on abortion in America did not come

from the general public or from the churches, which seemed content to remain quiet on the subject, perhaps out of the practical reason that abortion was going to happen whatever the rules. The first anti-abortion activity came from doctors, beginning with Percival. Mohr argues that abortion was a central element in the efforts of physicians to control their profession. "Regular" doctors—graduates from prestigious schools and members of medical associations that believed in "scientific medicine"—had grown increasingly alarmed since the turn of the century at their steady loss of patients and prestige to midwives, homeopaths, folk healers, or poorly educated doctors. In fact the regulars offered treatments that were often more dangerous and no more successful. Still, they had a profession to elevate, and abortion was going to be their lever.

Their motives were not entirely related to business. Mohr writes that the regular physicians "considered themselves the supreme champions of life as an absolute value, including fetal life. This was an important part of their ideology and it was embodied in the Hippocratic oath." Setting themselves up as moral authorities, the doctors were "bitterly disappointed" that the nation's main-line Protestant churches did not support them in their anti-abortion crusade of the post-Civil War era. In other words, the nation's Protestant majority, which reasonably could have seized abortion as a moral cause, did not.

Still, the physicians persisted. Many regulars railed against abortion among upper-class white women as a practice that would weaken the race purity of the country. They were also antifeminist. The more abortions there were, the less women would be forced to acknowledge that their proper place was in the home.

On the issue itself, most Americans believed that an unquick fetus was not a human being with rights. The regulars opposed abortion both before and after quickening. Claiming superior understanding of the issue based on science, they declared ignorant the notion that quickening was the beginning of life, because a fetus develops continuously from conception. And little by little, some states appeared to agree.

In 1840, Maine made abortion an offense "whether such child be quick or not." But the culpability fell only on the abortionist and the threat was weak: up to a year's imprisonment or a thousand-dollar fine, and there remained the loophole of proving intent. When the law came before the state supreme court in 1853, the judges freed an abortionist named Smith because his intent to abort could not be established—even though Smith had put a wire into the woman's uterine cavity and the woman had died! The court held that there were conceivably other medical purposes for his action.

Mohr puts it: "American courts were tolerant when an unquickened woman was treated for blocked menses"— the term of the day for a medical condition indistinguishable from early pregnancy. Mohr argues that *blocked menses* was more than a euphemism: Medical knowledge then provided no sure way to determine if a woman was pregnant before quickening. Yet it seems too that if the states were beginning to enact stricter laws, the application of those laws was still fairly loose.

In the twenty years between 1821 and 1841, ten states passed laws regulating abortion as part of their first laws regulating medicine. Yet abortion was not a notable public issue. All these statutes were included in omnibus bills, which meant that no legislator was on record voting on abortion alone; the abortion provisions were little noticed and rarely enforced. Five states made abortion a crime only after quickening and the remaining five had unenforceable laws. None made the women themselves culpable. The other sixteen of the twenty-six states then in the Union abided by the common law precedent of the 1812 Bangs case.

In the next forty years, however, due to the continued efforts of the medical profession, abortion would become a pressing American concern. The country appeared to adopt the nativistic thinking of the doctors. People who had been uninterested in the subject before now grew aware of a sharp rise in the number of abortions that had begun after 1830, especially among "white, married, Protestant, native born women of the middle and upper classes who either wished to delay their childbearing or already had all the children they wanted" (Mohr). Before then, abortions were generally to conceal unmarried or extramarital sex. The issue was becoming public.

Abortion went virtually unmentioned in the popular press before 1840. Now the arrest of an abortionist was a story for the dailies. A Madame Restell of New York City supervised a huge clinic there as well as branch agencies in Boston and Philadelphia. She employed a crew of road salesmen, who hawked her "female monthly pills" to restore "blocked menses." The salesmen were authorized to refer customers to the New York clinic if the pills failed. She was arrested twice, thus incurring great publicity that served her business well. "Female pills" like Madame Restell's were widely advertised, even in religious journals.

By midcentury, the physicians went all out. In 1857, Dr. Horatio Storer launched a national drive by the ten-year-old American Medical Association to eliminate abortion through state laws. The effect of these laws, however, was not to stop abortion altogether but to force women to gain the cooperation of a regular physician in order to abort. Although the physicians had a good deal to say about the role of women, abortion was not yet recognized as a feminist issue. Feminists of the time remained primarily concerned with avoiding death in childbirth and advocated intentional parenthood through sexual abstinence.

Protestant churches did gradually rally behind the doctors as their campaign peaked, in the late 1860s and early 1870s. And the Catholic Church, which had remained surprisingly silent on the issue, made its judgment known. In 1869, Pope Pius IX dismissed the "ensoulment" dividing line by extending excommunication to all those who aborted, not just those who aborted fetuses with souls.

By 1900, every state in the Union had passed a law forbidding the use of drugs or instruments to procure abortion at any stage of pregnancy, "unless the same be necessary to save the woman's life," in the opinion of a regular physician. Ten states required the concurrence of a second physician.

Thus American law implicitly represented the viewpoint that life began at conception. It explicitly stated that only a risk to the woman's life justified an abortion. Most importantly, the laws declared that doctors would decide who would abort and when. A personal or religious decision had become a medical one.

Perhaps as a result the laws were applied, as other laws had been before, with great latitude. The physicians were now secure in their professional concerns. Abortions were performed by American doctors after the post-Civil-War laws not only when the mother's life was in danger but when it was thought that the child might be deformed or a doctor was sympathetic to a woman's mental anguish, as in a case of pregnancy by rape. The lenient standards continued to be applied into the twentieth century. In the 1930s, poverty became a widely accepted basis for performing an abortion, despite the law. In the 1940s and 1950s, some doctors accepted psychiatric reasons for performing an abortion.

There were few indictments under these laws and even fewer convictions. Most abortions were illegal, often in dangerous circumstances. The safety and availability of abortion varied with individual circumstances. The poor and those in rural areas suffered the most. So went the situation, with anti-abortion laws in place, but increasing discomfort was felt by many people that those laws were working against real social needs. By midcentury it was hard to tell how strong the country's moral position was against abortion, but the moral opinion in favor of it was clearly growing.

The initiative to change the laws came again from

doctors, who this time were arguing in the opposite direction from their professional interest in the nineteenth century. In the 1950s doctors began complaining, correctly, that hospital review boards were restricting abortions against the better judgment of individual doctors. Medicine itself had grown bureaucratic, making the fifty-year system of legal condemnation and practical tolerance impractical.

In 1959 a society of jurists, lawyers, and scholars called the American Law Institute (ALI) suggested a standard abortion code. Its proposal outlined exactly which purposes justified an abortion and who would decide. An abortion would be permissible when pregnancy "would gravely impair the physical or mental health of the mother," if the child was likely to be born with "grave physical or mental defects," and in cases of pregnancy by rape or incest. The code required abortions to be approved by two doctors.

The American abortion liberalization movement gathered momentum through the 1960s, reaching a head in 1967. The year brought a rush of pro-choice activity, which coincided with the first stages of the women's movement. Betty Friedan led a group of the younger members of the one-year-old National Organization of Women to persuade its national conference to include the "right of Women to Control Their Reproductive Lives" in the NOW Women's Bill of Rights. The motion was passed only after intense debate—an early indication that attitudes differed even within the women's movement.

Yet support emerged among Protestant churches. The organization of American Episcopal bishops came out in favor of liberalized statutes in 1967; the American Baptist Convention did the same in 1968. Twenty-eight state legislatures considered reform bills based on the ALI code in the 1967 session alone. By 1973, thirteen states had passed them. Thus the answer to all three of abortion's basic questions—viability, justification, and the authority of decision—underwent total reversal.

One reason for the change in church attitudes as well as national attitudes was the 1962 Finkbine case, involving the likelihood of fetal deformity. Sherri Finkbine, a mother of four from Arizona, had scheduled a legal abortion at a local hospital after the doctor concluded that the fetus she was carrying was likely to be born deformed. She herself had discovered that the tranquilizer her husband had brought back for her from Europe was the same drug, called thalidomide, that had resulted in the births of children with flippers instead of arms, paralyzed faces, twisted legs, and missing ears. Although thalidomide had not been approved for sale in the U.S., it was generally available overseas.

Finkbine's life was never at risk. Yet the doctor and hospital agreed easily to her abortion, despite the fact that Arizona officially permitted abortions only to save the woman's life. It was not an unusual risk for either the doctor or hospital to take, so long as everyone involved kept quiet. Finkbine's case became a cause célèbre when she called the local newspaper to warn other American women against the foreign drug and the newspaper's front-page story persuaded the hospital to cancel the abortion. Finkbine tried a court challenge, but in the end she traveled to Sweden to obtain her abortion under its liberal law. The fetus was indeed deformed. A Gallup poll later found that 52 percent of those surveyed supported Finkbine, while 32 percent opposed her.

While special circumstances like Finkbine's aroused public interest, a growing number of feminists pursued a broader agenda. They argued that abortion was a woman's right, not only in the circumstances outlined in the ALI code but in general.

The British Parliament, which had been ahead of the United States in criminalizing abortion, now beat Americans in decriminalizing it. Its 1967 act, still in force, permitted abortion until viability with the certification of two doctors. Viability has been set at twenty-eight weeks. The British offered the interesting, permissive formula that abortion be legal if it is found to be safer than pregnancy. Since early abortion is generally safer than any pregnancy, the law permits abortion at will. There is a movement today in Britain to limit abortions to the first eighteen weeks.

Canada, after a period of gradual liberalization of its abortion statute based on the 1861 British one, took a fresh tack in 1969. Abortions could be induced if approved by three-member hospital committees to protect the life and health of the mother.

In 1970, Hawaii became the first U.S. state to repeal its abortion prohibition altogether rather than reform it along the ALI guidelines. The new law required no special hospital review procedure or parental consent, stipulating only that the abortion take place before "fetal viability." A Catholic governor signed the bill, saying that illegal abortions were dangerous and that legal silence on abortion respected the separation of church and state.

New York followed Hawaii the same year, legalizing abortions in the first twenty-four weeks. A particularly tough battle there pitted a feminist bloc against the Roman Catholic Church. The Church grew only more adamant in its opposition to abortion as the number of abortions increased. Pius XII, in the late 1940s and 1950s, had spoken tirelessly against abortion, rejecting any arguments that placed a higher value on the mother's life than that of the fetus, including arguments for therapeutic abortion. The Second Vatican Council listed abortion among such crimes as homicide, genocide, torture, slavery, and euthanasia. By the 1960s, the papal edicts on contraception and abortion seemed so contradictory to popular Catholic opinion that some theologians and bishops began to teach a theory of personal conscience, freeing Catholics to disobey Rome.

In New York, the Albany clerk was about to announce that the legalization bill had failed by one vote when an assemblyman representing a largely Catholic district approached the microphone with tears in his eyes and reversed his vote. Alaska followed in the same liberal direction as New York. Washington, after a popular referendum, permitted abortion in the first twenty weeks of pregnancy.

As of 1973, three states (Louisiana, New Hampshire, and Pennsylvania) prohibited abortion for any reason. Thirty-one states permitted abortion to save the woman's life. Thirty-four states held abortionists criminally liable; only nine also held the woman culpable. Thirteen states had reform laws modeled on the ALI code. Four (Alaska, Washington, New York, and Hawaii) permitted abortion for any reason before fetal viability or a cut-off point that varied from twenty to twenty-six weeks.

It is uncertain how far the nation would have gone in changing the abortion laws on a state-by-state basis. It is possible that the issue might have been taken up in the sort of public conversation I advocated in Chapter 1, but I doubt it. By the 1970s, the moral passions on abortion were running high, for reasons I will suggest in the next chapter. Those passions probably had to run their course before decelerating, as most of us hope they will. In any event, the Supreme Court preempted the process of state-by-state liberalization on January 22, 1973, when Justice Harry Blackmun, a Republican Nixon appointee, handed down the *Roe* v. *Wade* decision.

The decision was deemed so important that it had been argued twice, first in 1971, when it was "held over" to be reargued the next term. The Court in effect held that life began—at least in the legal sense of having rights—after fetal viability or six months; and that the woman had the unfettered right to choose an abortion in the first three months. The justifiable purposes of abortion were nobody's business but her own until then. During the "second trimester," from the third to the sixth month, abortions would be subject to government regulation to protect the woman's health (a separate issue from fetal rights).

The human story behind the legal case reveals something of the atmosphere of shame in which many women choose to abort. Jane Roe was a pseudonym for a woman who later publicly revealed herself as Norma McCorvey. (Henry Wade was the Dallas county prosecutor). She claimed that on a summer evening in 1969 she had been gang-raped while walking home from work. McCorvey was twenty-five years old and unmarried and did not have the money to travel outside the state for a legal abortion. She decided to challenge the Texas statute, which permitted abortion only in cases of life endangerment. More than a decade later, McCorvey would admit that the rape was a fabricated story to cover her shame at getting pregnant out of wedlock.

Also on January 22, 1973, the Supreme Court handed down a second abortion decision, *Doe* v. *Bolton*, concerning a Georgia statute. After she tried and failed to obtain an abortion, Mary Doe, a mother of three whose real name was Sandra Race Cano, gave birth to a daughter, whom she put up for adoption. The daughter and mother, who later met, are now on opposite sides of the abortion controversy. The surprise is that Cano has become a pro-life advocate and her daughter, Melissa Able, believes that Cano had a right to obtain the abortion she wanted.

Justice Blackmun argued in *Roe* that the Texas statute violated a woman's constitutional right to privacy, including, to quote one article, "a qualified right to abortion. The court did not hold that women had an absolute right to abortion. Instead, the court divided the pregnancy term into trimesters and held that in the first trimester, women had an unqualified right to privacy in deciding to abort . . .; in the second trimester, the state would adopt reasonable regulations pertaining to the mother's health; and in the third trimester, the state's interest in protecting the fetus was compelling enough to warrant complete proscription of abortion, except where the mother's life or health was endangered."

In *Doe* v. *Bolton*, the Court struck down a Georgia law based on the ALI code because it required a woman to follow an elaborate procedure, which included obtaining advance approval from a hospital committee. The justices decided by a vote of 7–2 that the procedural requirements violated her right to unfettered freedom to choose an abortion in her first trimester.

The two decisions together overturned the laws in every state, except New York, and in the District of Columbia. Many people denounced them as a preeminent example of judicial activism overstepping the prerogatives of state legislatures. The argument over political prerogatives could be described as a rider to our third basic question: Who decides who decides? Did courts have the right to hand the decision to individual women?

Four states (Indiana, Illinois, Louisiana, and South Dakota) registered their displeasure, passing laws after 1973 to allow for the automatic reenactment of their pre-1973 anti-abortion laws if *Roe* v. *Wade* were overturned. Except for Louisiana, which outlawed abortion for any reason, all permitted abortion only to save the woman's life. Some states, like Iowa, repealed and replaced their laws; others left unenforceable laws on the books. According to Tribe, "versions of these [post–Civil War] laws arguably remain on the books in more than thirty states today. . . . If *Roe* v. *Wade* were overruled, it will be urged that some of these laws—designed more to protect the medical profession than to safeguard either women or the unborn—will be enforceable even without reenactment by any twentieth-century legislature." But in early 1990, a Louisiana federal court ruled that the state's pre-Civil War anti-abortion statute had been implicitly repealed by later, inconsistent enactments and thus could not be enforced.

The privacy right enshrined in the landmark 1973 decisions would be upheld in subsequent decisions and would also be chipped away. In 1976, the Court held in two cases that states could not require a husband's or parent's consent as a condition of abortion; but in 1979 and 1983, it held that a state could require minors to obtain the consent of either a parent or a judge. Although parents could not have an absolute veto, neither did girls who were minors have an absolute right to decide. State laws could require parental consent so long as minors had a legitimate "judicial bypass" option—convincing a judge of their competence to choose an abortion.

The Court has also held that a woman's right to an abortion does not imply any governmental responsibility to fund one. The pro-life movement gathering steam after *Roe* v. *Wade* won its first significant battles on the funding issue. Since August 1977 (except for a brief interlude from February through September 1980), Congress prohibited the use of federal funds to provide abortions for women eligible for Medicaid (a program relying on both state and federal monies). The prohibitions have taken the form of annual "Hyde amendments," named for the original sponsor, Representative Henry J. Hyde, a Republican from Illinois. They are attached by Congress to the Department of Health and Human Services appropriations measure. The 1981 "Bauman amendment" allowed states to set their own funding policies stricter than the federal one.

In 1977, the Supreme Court upheld by a vote of 6 to 3 the right of states (and by implication the federal government) to refuse to spend public money for "elective" abortions. Thirty-seven states presently restrict Medicaid funding to cases of life endangerment; some of these also provide for cases of rape, incest, or fetal deformity.

In 1980, the Court voted 5 to 4 that it is constitutional for the federal government to offer Medicaid funding only to save the woman's life. Congress has legislated that federal funding be restricted to cases of life endangerment; the result is that very little in the way of Medicaid funds has actually been spent for abortions.

The *Roe* decision effectively shifted the abortion controversy to judicial appointments, court decisions, and efforts for a constitutional amendment. The pro-life forces have run into procedural opposition on constitutional grounds in trying to ban abortion through Congress. Senator Jesse Helms and Congressman Henry Hyde proposed a bill in 1981 to prompt the Supreme Court to reconsider *Roe*. Section 1 of the bill stated, "The Congress finds that . . . human life exists from conception," and that the fourteenth amendment protects human life. In 1983, the Senate Judiciary Committee heard testimony on a proposed pro-life constitutional amendment. Neither effort got any further. Nor did any anti-*Roe* action, until the *Webster* decision.

In short, what seems to have happened over our two hundred-year history is this: In the beginning we were headed toward more lenient abortion laws, content to live with the practical necessity of abortion and to avoid a discussion of its moral importance. Then the doctors, for professional advantages of their own, saw to it that restrictive laws were enacted. The churches then caught up with the doctors, though they too were initially content to look the other way when it came to abortion, because members of their congregations often needed abortions—a prudent tolerance. After the churches made their voices heard, however, abortion did become a moral issue, but it was not raised as such in public until the early 1900s, and even then the morality of the issue centered on the suffering of the poor in obtaining illegal abortions. Only in the 1960s, when women began to assert themselves and the doctors had changed their minds on abortion, did the issue begin to become a moral battleground. And once *Roe* v. *Wade* was decided, the war was on.

As it turned out, we have been at war for the past twenty-five years, and the war we have waged on this issue is greater than that of any other nation in history. Why we have been an anomaly is the next question. For the moment, consider that no society in history has ever figured out when a fetus is a person; none has ever determined when it is justifiable to abort a fetus; and none has ever settled the question of who decides. In short, the history of abortion is the history of conflict, and the nation most accustomed to living with conflicting problems has not been able to handle this one. Why?

Chapter 3

The American Anomaly

I began this book with the suggestion that we are closer in our thinking on abortion than the politics would indicate, but as yet we seem unable to live with the ambivalence the problem requires. The history of abortion, as encountered in Chapter 2, is a history of contradictory attitudes among various cultures; yet we, who are able to live in tension with a number of irreconcilable issues, have not profited from history's lesson in this regard, or from history's other lesson—that every society has suited its handling of abortion according to its special makeup. Our own historical experience with abortion has evolved into a divisive moral concern, which we have refused to articulate, thereby making it more difficult to treat abortion as one of our normal unresolvable problems. Before I offer a way to think of abortion as one of these normal problems, let me suggest why it has so abnormally confounded us.

To begin to answer why abortion has become such an explosive issue in recent years, it helps to appreciate (again) how peculiar a place America is in the scheme of world history and how peculiar the past twenty-five years have been, even for us. Earlier I mentioned that we seem to be the only civilization to have taken abortion so seriously as to engage in an emotional and intellectual civil war over the issue. But it must be said, to keep things in perspective, that we are the only civilization to do a lot of unusual things; and given the anomalous structure of our government and our population, it would be surprising if we hadn't taken an issue as potentially volatile as abortion and made it more rather than less difficult to deal with.

If there is a moral or ethical issue in the air capable of hurling one part of America against another part, the citizens will eventually seize it and make the most of it. This has been true of slavery, prohibition, civil rights, drugs, the youth culture, women's liberation, capital punishment, wars great and small; and it has been no less true of abortion. Why it took us as long as it did to focus on abortion as a moral issue may be due to the medical profession's assuming the issue as its own, thereby making it appear purely scientific, or to the fact that our feelings about abortion grew incrementally as the practice became more widespread. Yet we were bound to anguish over it eventually.

Americans, historically, are moral worriers. We tend to treat most every political issue that arises as a test of our national soul, because we are convinced that we are not happy unless we can turn a political disagreement into a monumental spiritual debate.

One reason for this is that America is, and always has been, a religious country, even though it spreads its religiosity among many different religions. Perry Miller, the great historian of American religious thought, established that the New England colonists arrived with a ready-made religious mission, which they cultivated and sustained through all its manifestations, from charity to intolerance. The Virginia settlement, too, was energized by God's glory. Nothing changed in this attitude by the time the nation was invented. If anything, the formal creation of the country made the desire to receive redemption in the New World more intense.

The idea of redemption has been both national and personal. In their anthology of Puritan writings *The Puritans in America*, Alan Heimert and Andrew Delbanco observe that in coming to the New World, the Puritans were immediately transformed from a minority to the majority, from a hounded sect in one country to the dominant voice of political and moral authority in another. Thus empowered, and lacking external enemies, they turned upon themselves in an effort to purify their own. Deviants from the orthodoxy were rooted out, and the sect, now the ruling class, nurtured the strict codes and cultural severity by which it has always been known.

Yet within that stern and passionless structure individuals still sought something in American religion that was different, more emotional than the religion practiced in England. One member of an early congregation explained that the reason he made the long journey to America was, "I thought I should find feelings." The promise, while imprecise, was strongly felt by many— that in the New World one might discover or revive one's personal relationship with God. The challenges involved with saving one's soul quickly became a matter to be settled between oneself and one's maker.

This personalized sense of religion has an odd but telling relationship with the national attitude toward religion. Officially, America is an areligious country; the separation of church and state is so rooted in the democracy it has become a cliché. Yet that same separation has created and intensified a hidden national feeling about faith and God, a sort of secret, undercurrent religion, the tenets of which surface whenever moral questions go public.

In *Under God*, Garry Wills's study of religion and politics in America, the case of Gary Hart's sexual escapades during the presidential campaign of 1988 is offered as an example of how the country, when exposed to an obvious moral issue (i.e., adultery), will do its best to discuss it in digressive terms such as *character* or *values*. The avoidance, strained and deliberate, signals the intensity of feelings about the moral issue. The moralizing Church Lady on the *Saturday Night Live* TV show is popular because "she" is funny; but she is funny because, as a zealot, she is widely recognizable.

In December 1990, *Life* magazine ran a cover that put forward the question "Who is God?" In the article, respondents from all over the world offered personal answers to the question. The issue sold over seven hundred thousand copies, making it the second highest seller of the year. (The first, incidentally, was the issue with a cover showing photographs of the initial stages of the growth of the fetus.) The depth and extent of spiritual feeling and belief in this country is vast. It shows up in the opinion polls, in the number of houses of worship in any community, and in the variety of religions. It shows up in one's private ruminations.

Something about the size, the insistent mobility, or the heterogeneity of America has given the country its special, subterranean religious feeling. The smallest incident can bring that feeling to the fore. The largest and most complex moral problem, such as abortion, can confound it for decades.

The more recent reason for our generating a storm over abortion, I believe, is that for the past twenty-five years or so, America has not been a country with a consensus on anything. Perhaps this sort of working chaos in which we function was inevitable as soon as the Statue of Liberty showed her torch to the seas. But until the 1960s, a general if tenuous image of homogenized middle-class American life sustained itself. Even the European immigrants of the late nineteenth and twentieth centuries, who, had they wanted to, could have usurped the status quo, wound up aspiring to it and reinforcing it. The Protestant majority established a standard of thought and conduct and the newcomers agreed to live by it.

That all began to fall apart visibly around 1965. In an astonishingly short period, America went from a country of unified and conventional dreams to one divided bitterly about such issues as Vietnam, poverty, women, race, and law and order. The country shifted from *Mr. Bland-ings Builds His Dream House* to *Wild in the Streets.* Communities disintegrated, families became generational war zones, marriages dissolved.

"We look out on this world of 1969 as a deeply divided country," wrote Hedley Donovan, editor-in-chief of Time, Inc., whose predecessor, Henry Luce, had announced the advent of "the American Century" only twenty-five years earlier. "It is easy to say that it is the cruel question of Vietnam that has got us mixed up. But I believe the causes of our confusion go much deeper. [We have] the loss of a working consensus, for the first time in our lives, as to what we think America means."

A nation at once committed to diversity and to the validity of everyone's opinion was bound to reach a point of no consensus from the start. Easier to accept the idea of pluralism than its consequences, and one of its consequences since the 1960s was that America might never think as a single entity on important issues again. In 1989, twenty years after Donovan's observation, university curriculums began to come apart along ethnic lines because certain people in authority wanted to change the focus of higher learning from those called DWEMS, Dead White European Males, such as Shakespeare and Mozart, toward a host of ethnic directions. In a sense, the DWEMS stood for the Cabots, Lodges, and Smiths of the former national majority.

Perhaps no event of the late 1960s was more meaningful in terms of shaking up America than the women's movement. This movement had existed for a long while, but quietly; now, as the country reached the height of anti-Vietnam protests in 1968 and 1969, the women's movement rekindled. One odd reason for its revival, in fact, was that women were generally excluded from leadership in the antiwar movement.

With the radicalization of women came disruptions of established conditions that have only increased and grown more complicated in recent years. The addition of women in the workforce, even now, when it is clearly an economic necessity for most families, still causes concern to many men that their power is being usurped. Women, too, are concerned that their desire to succeed as workers collides with an equal desire to succeed as wives and mothers. Such problems are old hat now, but they do not go away; and in the late 1960s they augured enormous schisms in American society. Obviously, the increased strength and dignity of women pertained directly to their freedom in the matter of abortion.

Not coincidentally, the year 1969 marked the beginning of the pro-life movement, a full four years before *Roe* v. *Wade*. The movement may have started because the doctors were no longer on the pro-life side or because women were claiming their rights. But abortion was also a pure moral question to many; and one of the interesting characteristics of the pro-life movement when it began was that it was relatively selfless, as political movements go. Pro-lifers were fighting for the rights of the "unborn."

Comparatively their battle started small. With everything else that was driving the country apart in the late 1960s one hardly noticed abortion, much less suspected that it would soon establish itself as the most divisive

issue of the lot. Yet few of the other points of friction
would prove as durable, and none, with the possible exception of race, would prove as personally painful and
complicated.

One hard look at the country's response to victory in
the Persian Gulf war at the beginning of 1991 reaffirmed
the deep national divisions, which have persisted, though
the picture appeared to be otherwise. All the televised
celebrations, all the cheering for the returning soldiers,
the parades, the statements of the politicians, were not
enough to keep buried the buried truth that America is
not a country of shared goals anymore. The simplicity of
an easy victory over Iraq presented a moment's relief
from that unhappy knowledge. But the celebration was
an emotional game the country created for itself. When
the flag waving would eventually stop, America would be
as fractured as it was before Saddam Hussein gave it a
breather of forgetfulness.

These two phenomena—America's basic religiosity
and the absence of a consensus in the country—provide
the frames of reference in which it is possible to understand why abortion troubles Americans as deeply as it
does. The other reasons lie in specific characteristics of
American thought, each of which has proved especially
volatile when abortion has come in contact with it. Each
of these commonly recognized national characteristics
has been used by both pro-life and pro-choice believers as
proof of the rightness of their cause.

The characteristics are the following: individualism,
optimism, a preoccupation with evil, and a dogged middle-
classness, especially as regards sexuality. I will take the

characteristics up one by one and try to suggest how each characteristic has become peculiarly explosive when abortion has touched it.

~~~~

For an idea so universally acknowledged as to be commonplace, American individualism goes awfully deep and extends to some very mysterious places. Individualism was not invented in America—the Industrial Revolution freed other Western nations from the bonds of caste and class. But individualism was invented *with* America, the two ideas coming into being at the same time in the late eighteenth and early nineteenth centuries. Since that time they have been inseparable, to the point that one does not think of the American character without reference to the prominence and power of the independent mind and person.

That prominence and power have taken various forms, some of which are antithetical to others. Emerson, the evangelist of self-reliance and nonconformity, had a quasi-mystical sense of the value of the self. He described "man" as a self-sufficient microcosm: "The lightning which explodes and fashions planets, maker of planets and suns, is in him." Tocqueville had a more prosaic and practical view. He worried about the tendency of Americans to withdraw into themselves at the expense of the public good, confusing self-assertion with self-absorption.

Abortion hits both of these views of the individual head-on, of course; but both views are open to antipodal interpretations. The Emersonian celebration of the individual, which is merely a fancier version of the American pioneer, may be shared by the pro-choice advocate who sees in individualism one's right to privacy. It may be seen equally by a pro-life advocate as a justification for taking an individual stance—an antiliberal stance to boot—on a matter of conscience.

The idea of the independent individual may also be embraced by the pro-life position as the condition of life on which the unborn have a claim immediately after conception. Pro-life advocates see the pregnant woman as two individuals, each with an equal claim to the riches that American individualism offers.

Tocqueville's concern with individualism as selfishness is also available for adoption by both camps. The pro-life people claim that the pro-choice advocates are placing their definition of individual rights above those of society; and one of the fundamental rights of American society is the right to life. Even the Supreme Court, when it passed *Roe*, concluded that abortion "is not unqualified and must be considered against important state interests in regulation."

To those who believe in abortion rights, the "public good" consists of a society in which people, collectively, have the right to privacy and individual choice. Their vision of an unselfish, unself-centered America is one in which the collective sustains its strength by encouraging the independence of those who comprise it. Logically, both camps rail against the individual imposing his or her individual views on society at large, each feeling the same, if opposite, passion about both what society and the individual ought to be.

Ironies fly all around these debates, which serve to intensify them. The same people who chide pro-choice advocates for self-interested individualism are often those who actively oppose other forms of collective good—social programs for the poor, the ignorant, and the disadvantaged. The pro-choice people who seize upon individual rights are often those who fight for collectivity in those same social programs. It is not that the people on both sides do not realize these contradictions in their thinking. But they do not give them much weight intellectually. They tend to put abortion in a special room in their minds, perhaps because the issue involves the body and other mysteries like sex and love and thus seems removed from the demands of intellectual consistency.

Yet it is in that private room of thought that abortion and individualism have their most terrible collisions. Americans rarely think of themselves as compendiums of national characteristics; they see themselves as people. They want to live properly as people, and often they define the country as themselves writ large. If they acknowledge a connection between America and themselves, it is to see America *as* themselves. That private room of thought is also a public square, the Senate chamber, the Supreme Court.

The basis of that imaginative projection, however, is still a very lonely perch. And the reason abortion affects the idea of American individualism so deeply is that life in America is for the most part lonely and isolated. Loneliness is the dark side of independence, often the penalty for independence. Americans, more than other people, perhaps *because* of the absence of a state religion, are thrown upon themselves to make major moral decisions. When an issue as complicated as abortion surfaces—whether it involves oneself, one's daughter, or a total stranger—it hits American loneliness with special force.

The sense of our aloneness is both personal and national. America started out as a separate idea in the world of nations, was indeed created out of an impulse for separation. Once it was created, the early colonists attempted to make a reconnection with the Old World by striving to become a spiritual model for it, a corrective for what Cotton Mather called the "Depravations of Europe." When the first New Englanders failed to establish such a model, they were more alone still.

"They looked in vain to history for an explanation of themselves," wrote Perry Miller in *Errand Into the Wilderness*, his brilliant and comprehensive study of America's spiritual past. "Thereupon these citizens found that they had no other place to search but within themselves . . . Having failed to rivet the eyes of the world upon their city on the hill, they were left alone with America."

We have always been thus. When it turns out from time to time that our conduct is singularly different from that of the rest of the world, as it has been over abortion, the fact does not really surprise us. The American way of individualism calls on us to solve our own problems our own way. And when an issue such as abortion takes hold, one that might allow us to profit from the experience of other countries and from the past, we turn away and inward simultaneously. The results of all that collective introspection are displayed in shouting matches, riots, and demonstrations.

There may be another aspect of individualism connected with abortion—though I admit that it may be a stretch. Since America and Americans know, and to an extent are defined by, isolation, we have an acute appreciation of the state of the orphan. The country began as an orphan, and later became an orphan by choice, albeit the world's most powerful baby, like Gargantua. The idea of the child alone, with whom we naturally sympathize, may affect the views of abortion in one of two ways. Those who approve of abortion detest the prospect of the unwanted, isolated child. Those who condemn it see the isolated, unprotected child as vulnerable in the womb.

Privacy is an admirable idea, but since it is not granted along with omniscience, it may also create terrors. The great majority of citizens, who, while favoring abortion rights, are nonetheless confused and troubled by the issue, do not find their confusion eased by the fact that they are independent individuals. On their own, in solitary ruminations, they must work their way through the problem. This is certainly preferable to receiving a simplistic, doctrinaire word from a church or other authoritarian source, but it is a lot more difficult to deal with and only emphasizes the solitary nature of American citizenship.

One reason abortion has so deeply troubled America is that it has troubled individual Americans, whose nationality is largely defined by the right to brood on their own. We are alone in a lonely country; we are alone with ourselves; the act of conception produces a being alone. To ponder these interacting solitudes understandably could result in a rage of confusions. It has.

~~~~~

The American characteristic of optimism, like that of individualism, is affected by abortion in contradictory ways. People favoring the pro-life position see optimism exactly as they read individual rights: Every American, born or unborn, is entitled to look forward to a state of infinite hope and progress. The process of birth is itself an optimistic activity. A country charged to bear fruit and multiply without impediment satisfies a domestic manifest destiny to become "the last best hope of men on earth." Those words were Jefferson's, but they were quoted most often by Ronald Reagan, who openly opposed abortion rights and was generally seen as America's apostle of optimistic thought.

Taking the opposite view, those favoring abortion rights interpret the ideas of hope and progress as a consequence of one's entitlement to free choice in all things, abortion definitely included. If the individual woman wishes to pursue her manifest destiny unencumbered by children she does not want, that is not only her business but her glory. The issue is national as well as personal. The pro-choice reasoning goes: The country may only reach its ideal goals if women, along with men, are allowed to achieve their highest potential as citizens, unencumbered by limitations not of their own choosing.

Also, the country may only reach its goals if its population is kept under control, welfare rolls are shortened, and the number of unwanted children is held to a minimum. The fewer the children, the more money there is to go around. Since American optimism and money are blood brothers, abortion can just as logically be seen and embraced as part of the American dream as it can be shunned as the American nightmare.

Two conflicting views of progress are at play here: One is that progress is always to be reckoned as good; the other is that it may represent a loss of essential spiritual values or the triumph of a stampeding civilization over nature. Both views, oddly, involve optimism, but of opposite sorts. One looks backward to America as a pristine state of nature, in which the very existence of a wilderness corresponded to America's expansive hopes. The other looks forward to America as the house of industry and invention, in which the best of America may be realized by paving the wilderness with parking lots.

Abortion, ever malleable, fits comfortably with both views. To give birth is to engage in an act of nature, whereas the mechanism of abortion, an instrument of progressive civilization, is a contradiction, a destruction of natural life. Yet both views of progress are optimistic; they merely involve different optimistic views of the same country. The real and true America, says one camp, is that which holds to the old-fashioned values of the land. The real and true America, says the other camp, is that which commands the future with inventiveness. In one sense, this contest of views is part of the eternal conflict between the country and the city.

Yet both camps see into the life of the other, and to some degree they believe in that opposing life. The citified, industrial mind longs for rural values; the agrarian mind wants city goods and city machines. Abortion may be a blessing to an overlarge rural family, just as it may be a source of deep moral turbulence in an urban upper-middle-class family that chooses the procedure for social convenience.

This issue of American inventiveness, a cornerstone of America's optimism, is very tricky when it comes to abortion. Abortion is not an American invention, of course, but in many ways it appeals to Americans like any invention—a technological procedure by which the life of a woman may be happily simplified and enhanced. Less work for mother, if one wants to put it coldly.

It is difficult to overestimate the appeal of inventiveness for its own sake in this country. Perhaps because the country itself was invented, the mere idea of forging something new, especially something mechanical that outdoes a function of nature, has always had a gripping effect on the American imagination. As if born to make everything over, the country—as soon as it was a country—promoted the social status of craftsmen and artisans to that of the highest statesmen. At celebrations of the ratification of the Constitution, craftsmen were honored as national leaders. In a Boston ratification parade in January 1788, artisans and mechanics joined in a procession led by John Hancock, who rode in a vehicle pulled by thirteen "patriotic mechanics," followed by Paul Revere in a four-horse sleigh.

What the earliest Americans saw in themselves as builders of the new, others in the world, the older world, confirmed. A scientist writing in a French medical journal in 1787 declared: "The discovery of America has not only been an interesting spectacle for politics and ambition, it has opened a new field to human knowledge; it has furnished new wealth to all parts of natural history. . . . Everything is new in America, everything seems to have been arranged there after a different plan from that which provided at the formation of the rest of the earth."

With such spectacular reviews added to its own built-in ebullience, it is a small wonder that the country has always believed that it was capable of remaking all that was ever made before, including life itself. It seems not at all surprising that the Mary Shelley Frankenstein myth of the reinvented man, the life made new from dead parts, took hold in America much more than it did in Europe. The same basic attraction to and fascination with the idea of reproducing life undergirded much of American fiction and science fiction. Hawthorne's short story "The Artist of the Beautiful" is about a man who invented a mechanical butterfly as beautiful as the real thing.

Americans are capable of making anything. That is what the country has continued to believe even in the face of such soul-wrenching menaces and disappointments as the Russian Sputnik and Japanese cars. The nation's automatic reaction to those assaults on its destiny, after a frozen moment of fright, was to race like hell to make sure that it would overtake anyone threatening to wrest command of the new from its hands.

Most of all, Americans can make themselves. This belief harkens back to the country's faith in individualism; it sees the individual as an invention, the idea of the "self-made man" being almost literal. Perry Miller saw the entire character of the country as an inventive procedure: "Being an American is not something inherited but something to be achieved." With brains and imagination, or pluck and luck, Americans can manufacture whole lives for themselves, whole dynasties.

And they can unmake life, too, when life seems an impediment to progress and growth.

The invention of abortion, like other instruments of American optimism, cuts both ways. Hail the procedure as something that allows women to realize full control over their invented selves. Or damn the procedure as that which destroys forever the possibility of a new life inventing itself. As with all else pertaining to this issue, one's moral position depends on the direction in which one is looking. Yet both directions are heaving with optimism, and both see life in America as the best of choices.

~~~~

The faith of America's optimism, as strong as it is, is equaled by the fear and acknowledgment of evil forces within the country and the American character. America has always been as prone to darkness as to light, both in its thoughts and actions. Responding to the assassination of President Kennedy, Henry Steele Commager, whose vision of American history is grandly patriotic, said nonetheless that the country was "beset by division and the spectacle of hatred, and shaken by pervasive guilt."

Senator William Fulbright added in a speech: "It may be that the nation as a whole is healthy and strong and entirely without responsibility for the great misfortune that has befallen it. It would be comforting to think so. I for one do not think so. I believe that our society, though in most respects decent, civilized and humane, is not, and never has been, entirely so. Our national life, both past and present, has also been marked by a baleful and incongruous strand of intolerance and violence."

The responses to the forces of malevolence only increased in the 1960s; first there was the assassination of President Kennedy in 1963, then the Martin Luther King and Robert F. Kennedy assassinations in 1968. The 1960s were a decade in which the country was repeatedly reminded of its destructive side: in the clashes of the generations; in the proliferation of drugs; in the killings and race riots; and perhaps especially in Vietnam, which was regarded by many as a race war, a display of savagery against a people of different color. Depictions of that war, in such films as *Apocalypse Now* and *Full Metal Jacket,* reinforced the view of that war as a monstrous, quasi-supernatural evil.

That abortion rose as a major issue in the 1960s is, I believe, connected to the acknowledgment of America's darker impulses. Yet again, as with previously described characteristics, the perception of evil in the culture affected abortion in two opposing ways.

The pro-choice people saw the restriction of abortion as the evil in the culture. America was revealing its sinister side by creating a situation in which the abortionist was a criminal and the woman seeking an abortion was a participant in a crime—a crime committed in dark and dangerous places. The pro-life side saw abortion itself as the evil within the country's heart, and they condemned the practice as another massacre of innocents in the nation's history.

However often the country has been involved in the massacre of innocents, it is also aware of its guilt in such matters. The guilt reflects its good side, the massacres its bad. Richard Slotkin's fascinating book about the mythology of the American frontier, *Regeneration Through Violence*, points out that America is divided in its self-estimation as either enlightened or steeped in darkness. From the nation's start, writes Slotkin:

The antimythologists of the American Age of Reason believed in the imminence of a rational republic of yeoman farmers and enlightened leaders living amicably in the light of natural law and the Constitution. They were thereby left unprepared when the Jeffersonian republic was overcome by the Jacksonian democracy of the western man-on-the-make, the speculator, and the wildcat banker; when racist irrationalism and a falsely conceived economics prolonged and intensified slavery in the teeth of American idealism; and when men like Davy Crockett became national heroes by defining national aspiration in terms of so many bears destroyed, so much land preempted, so many trees hacked down, so many Indians and Mexicans dead in the dust.

That divided nature was the subject of much of the nation's early literature—the horrors of Poe, the moral menaces of Hawthorne and Melville.

Yet the light and the dark impulses of the culture are not secrets from each other. In modern America, especially since Vietnam (though slavery and lynchings provided the truth long before), one openly acknowledges that the country is indeed capable of terrible violence, that a strain of murderousness is as much a part of the national temper as are the strains of democracy, egalitarianism, or even optimism. The inner-city children, children as young as ten and eleven, who regularly kill one another with easily acquired handguns provide a shocking symbol of national contradictions.

This fusion of creative power and destructive power relates directly to the country's responses to abortion. Pro-life people, who are often, ironically, pro-war and pro-capital punishment people too, nonetheless see abortion as evidence of the dark and murderous side of the American mind. Pro-choice people, when they think of the fetus as a life, often sympathize with the revulsion of the pro-life side. It is not mere melodrama that makes a pro-life propaganda film like *The Silent Scream,* a graphic depiction of a late-stage abortion, effective in its repellence. A great many Americans see abortion as murder. They reconcile their personal morality to the act, as do soldiers in a war, by also believing that sometimes killing is necessary for a greater good.

Underneath that rationality, however, Americans believe most strongly that they possess a soul, one that is in constant danger of damnation, contamination, or merely losing its way. Other countries identify and cultivate national souls as well, but never, seemingly, with our alert sense of trepidation. The smallest event that involves the country is met with prolonged discussions of whether America's soul is as pure as it ought to be, whether the country is retaining its moral sights and so forth. As determined as Americans are to pursue individual paths toward independent goals and destinies, we fuss about our collective soul as if we were guardians of a potential monster.

All this fearful attention probably derives from the knowledge of our proven power to dominate life. Americans carved and hacked a progressive civilization out of a wilderness to acquire terrestrial goods—better homes, gardens, and everything. The more we gained of the material world, the more we hankered for the spiritual. Or we always said that we did. Or we apologized for not doing so. Yet nothing ever deterred for long our lust for power over the natural world in the vast and continuous national effort to control our fate.

The literal domination of life that the practice of abortion entails suits American values exactly. Yet the nation's vigilance over its soul has served as a counter impulse. In abortion, many Americans see a titanic struggle between national creativity and national destructiveness, and they find themselves torn about the issue not only personally but as citizens of a land whose history has heaved drastically between extremes of creativity and destructiveness from the beginning.

Ever since the first Pilgrims caught sight of the shore, Americans have wondered whether in the New World they were about to discover heaven or hell; we are wondering about that still. Unlike Milton's Satan in *Paradise Lost*, who was able to comfortably mix his hells and heavens, this country does not adjust its thoughts so easily and thus swings as severely between self-celebration and self-hate as it does between acts that might justify either reaction. Perhaps no people in history ever wanted so desperately to be good, morally good.

Perhaps for that reason the idea of evil is extremely powerful in this country. And the depiction of abortion as an evil affects those who favor abortion rights almost as much as those who contest them. Americans, who have known and practiced evil in their history, are excessively conscious of their darker capacities. Whether or not they approve of the practice, abortion reminds them of those darker capacities.

~~~~

The connection of abortion with American attitudes toward sexuality is both economic and mystical, the first obviously being easier to explain than the second. The American way with sex is directly related to the country's original desire to become a society of the middle class and thus to cast off the extremes of luxury and poverty that characterized Europe and the Old World. The structure of English society in particular was something the new nation sought to avoid. Not for Puritan America was the rigid English class system, which not only fixed people into economically immobile slots but allowed and encouraged free-wheeling sexual behavior at both the highest and lowest strata.

At the top of the English classes was a self-indulgent minority rich enough to ignore middle-class moral codes and idle enough to spend their time seducing servants. The privileged order looked upon the lower orders as having been created for their pleasure; they believed that they had inborn rights to abuse them. The figure of the eighteenth-century or Victorian libertine nobleman, while something of a caricature, is most frequently represented by his wanton seduction of poor, helpless girls.

At the opposite end of the system, the poor also felt free to do whatever they wished with their bodies, since the world offered them so little and they had nothing to lose by leading lives of dissolution. The masses of urban poor, created by the Industrial Revolution, had little or no hope of bettering their lot. Many of them wallowed in a kind of sexual Pandemonium, producing babies wantonly and routinely engaging in rape and incest. Between the two class extremes stood the staunch English middle class, with its hands on its hips, outraged at the behavior both above and below them but powerless to insist on, much less to enforce, bourgeois values.

This, of course, was not the case in America, where bourgeois values were to become the standards and the moral engine of the country. Puritanism, a mere aberrant religion to the English, which they were able to get rid of in 1660 after a brief eighteen years, was the force that dominated American social life for a century and a half. Since there has been a natural progression from Puritanism to Victorianism and from Victorianism to modern forms of fundamentalism in terms of social values, it may be said that the Puritans have really never loosened their headlock on American thinking. The Puritans offered a perfect context for America's desire to create a ruling middle class, which was to be known equally for infinite mobility (geographic, social, economic) and the severest forms of repression.

An irony of the American middle class is that while it fervently preached personal autonomy and laissez-faire capitalism, it also represented the most repressive people sexually. Conversely, those who have preached economic and political collectivism and condemned laissez-faire thinking have often been the most sexually liberated.

The appetite for sexuality was and is still the most prominent object of the middle-class repressive impulse. One basis for the repression of American sexuality is money. Sexual repression encourages conformity, conformity encourages domestic values. In profligate societies, where children were brought into the world helter-skelter, the lines of inheritance were confused and society was made disorderly. Monogamy, on the other hand, made for a clean and stable society; and in early America, where women were scarce and settlers needed both helpmates and children, a monogamous system ensured balance and promoted growth.

It was thus reasonable that an economic force or justification should become a moral voice, as morals and money were proved to be interdependent. To this day, Americans who stray too far from the social insistences of the ruling middle class are ostracized privately and publicly. Unchecked or deviant sexual behavior in America is a sin against the basic, and generally successful, economic order, which has created the only true community of agreement in this country. To get ahead in America, one must acknowledge and live by, or appear to live by, an assumed code of respectability. The Puritans were concerned with God's damnation, but even God's damnation soon paled compared with the terrestrial rejection of one's peers.

Abortion fits into such thinking more by what the issue implies than by what it may be in fact. As the previous chapter's discussion of the history of the issue suggested, Americans were able to live with abortion, even during periods of intense national prudery, as long as the practice was considered the exception that proved the rule. The rule was that abortion was legally and morally discouraged. Indeed, most every civilization has adopted that attitude, which, put simply, is an attitude of looking the other way in a difficult human situation that often cannot and should not be avoided. For all our adamant middle-classness, it was not uncomfortable for Americans to look the other way, either—at least until recently.

When, thanks to the medical profession, abortion was no longer allowed to be a private, albeit dangerous business, America's basic middle-classness asserted itself loudly. Who was having all these abortions? The upper classes, who were behaving irresponsibly, and the lower orders, who had nothing to lose. Abortion, in other words, was a sign of careless sexuality and was thus an offense to the bourgeois dream.

Was it also an offense or a threat to American economic growth? It hardly seemed so, if the decreased number of unwanted children kept the welfare rolls down. Yet there is always the assumption in this country that more is better for the economy. A popular complaint against the rich, if they delimit the number of children they have, if they have any at all, is that they are forfeiting progeny in order to pursue self-indulgent lives. To deny the existence of children is seen as anti-expansion, thus anti-American.

The main complaint, however, is that abortion contradicts middle-class values, which dictate the rules of sexual conduct. Abortion, it is assumed, is the practice of the socially irresponsible, those who defy the solid norms that keep America intact. When *Roe* v. *Wade* was ruled upon, it sent the harshest message to the American middle class, including those within that class who did not oppose abortion, that their conventions were not being respected. Those who did not oppose abortion nonetheless did oppose the disruption of conformity and stability. If the middle-class majority did not object to *Roe* v. *Wade* specifically, they did very much object to the atmosphere of lawlessness or unruliness that they felt the law encouraged.

They objected to abortion especially at a time when everything else in American life seemed to be spinning out of control. Since the late 1960s, sexuality had been used as a weapon against the American middle class. Free sex, much like long hair and drugs, constituted a political assault on conventional behavior. Advertisements for open sex in the underground press and televised pictures of bare-breasted women at the Woodstock rock festival were ways of saying that the emerging generation intended to bring the establishment down. Permissible abortion was part of the attack.

In short, *Roe* v. *Wade* made even those who were solidly pro-choice more than a little nervous about the prospect of a destabilized society. If one had to be for instability by being for abortion, the choice was Hobson's.

The mystical element in America's attitude toward sexuality, while harder to pin down historically, has even a stronger connection to the country's abortion furor. For one reason or another, America has been almost antibiological in its fear and loathing of sex—at least in its outward fear and loathing. H. L. Mencken blamed such odd attitudes on "the inherent Puritanism of the people—that conviction of the pervasiveness of sin, of the supreme importance of moral correctness, of the need of savage and inquisitorial laws [that have] been a dominating force in American life since the very beginning."

A puritanical outlook about sex certainly prevailed in the eighteenth and nineteenth centuries. In England as well as America, the paths of lust and lechery led to the inevitable consequences of the "Rake's Progress." In the words of Oliver Goldsmith's poem, "when lovely woman stoops to folly," the only moral choice was "to die."

In America the puritanism of the middle class became the controlling and the legal voice in all matters sexual. In nearly every state, sexual intercourse was prohibited for unmarried minors and was classified as "delinquent behavior." For those of age who were unmarried, such behavior became the crime of "fornication," punishable by fines or prison or both. Even today about half the states have statutes classifying fornication as a crime subject to penalties that range from a ten-dollar fine in Rhode Island to a possible thousand-dollar fine in Florida, along with a one-year prison term. Such "savage and inquisitorial laws" are rarely enforced, but as yet no one has felt the enlightened urge to remove them.

Yet the country's official abhorrence of sex cannot be attributed solely to the Puritan fathers' historical dread of sin. By the nineteenth century, most Americans, except those obsessed with Calvinistic self-recrimination, did not seriously believe that a night of making whoopie led straight to hell. There was still, however, the terrestrial hell of the opinions of society to deal with. The concern about the judgment of one's peers—a concern as strong today as it ever was—regulated sexual conduct as strictly as any firebrand minister.

Susan B. Anthony, a celebrated pioneer in women's rights, recalled that her mother would go into seclusion when each of her children was about to be delivered. Her grandmother would quietly and discreetly prepare all the necessary garments and bring them to the house, and nothing would ever be said about the event. The implication was that the act of giving birth was either a shame in itself or the consequence of a shame. One simply was not to look at sex in any of its manifestations or stages or to talk of it or in fact to acknowledge its existence.

Abortion not only acknowledges that sexual activity exists; it implies that it exists in a careless and illicit climate. Those who opposed abortion before *Roe* v. *Wade* seemed clearly to worry more about the illegality of sexual intercourse than about the illegality of abortion. What was illegal was, of course, improper, not up to the correct standards of society. The whole idea of abortion is upsetting to many Americans not because of the practice itself but because the subject opens a door to a realm of behavior that they simply do not wish to think about.

Why this should be so, why Americans are ahistorical in their approach to sex as in so much else, can be traced, I believe, to the country's primary aims and ambitions. This country started out as a place more of the mind than of the body. America was born not of history but of philosophy, and the natural tendency of the citizens is to think their way into experience. That America is also anti-intellectual in many ways is ironic but not really contradictory. Americans favor men of action over men of thought, Brom Bones over Ichabod Crane, but the man of action is himself the embodiment of a philosophy. His freedom of thought and movement represents the realization of a country built upon and sustained by ideas.

Where those ideas of freedom lead are to prosperity; that has been proved over the years. The odd notions of Puritanism would never have lasted as long as they did had they not been validated by an abundant and prosperous nation. The idea that philosophy leads to prosperity creates a purposeful and directed society, one that abjures not only hedonism but leisure. (Recall how short-lived was all the talk of "leisure time," so popular fifteen years ago.) Americans were born free to work, and the rewards of life accrue to work.

It doesn't take much to see how basically sexless such an atmosphere is. Americans who travel abroad to exotic, tropical places light up like glowworms at the sight of cultures sexually uninhibited. This country does anything but celebrate sexuality; it hides it; it may not even like it very much. One reason there is so much sex in the office in America is that the office at least presents a practical excuse and context for a purely pleasurable activity: a little business, a little fooling around.

A scene in the movie *Network* illustrates it all perfectly. Faye Dunaway, a hysterically ambitious TV producer, is in the midst of copulating with William Holden, an older TV executive. She is on top of him, and as she pumps up and down, groaning and sweating, she never stops talking about the show they plan to do together— the profits, the audience share. The American way of sex is ideally realized in the coupling of love and money.

That most of the nation's dirty jokes are thought to originate among the denizens of Wall St. makes the same connection.

Abortion does not simply remind America that sex exists out of wedlock; it reminds the country that sex exists period. One would think that the country would need no such reminders, but sexual activity of any sort has always had to sneak into the culture; it is never greeted openly. The titillation that slyly welcomes girlie magazines, cable TV sex shows, or telephone numbers to be dialed for romance is soon quashed by legislation; and the public at large, the same public that was titillated, never objects to the quashing. Indeed, the people seem to feel that they ought to be punished for impure or deviant thoughts—Jimmy Carter's lust in the heart.

Underlying all this is the American view of women, which embraces the virgin and the whore with equal fervor. For decorum's sake, the country promotes the virgin and hides the whore; or to be less censorious, it hides, denies the idea of woman as sex object, consigning that image to movie vamps. Odd as it is to say, in late twentieth-century America the established attitude, contradicted by all evident practice, is still that nice girls don't do it.

Nice girls, however, do become wives and mothers. That is the best way to preserve our middle-classness. The woman who does not wish to become a wife or mother is an implicit threat to "normal" society. The vehemence with which pro-life men and women often attack pro-choice women is, I believe, connected to that feeling of threat. Ironically, the free woman in America represents a criticism of America; the country will not abide her.

When the Kinsey report (*Sexual Behavior in the Human Male*, by Alfred C. Kinsey, Wardell B. Pomeroy, and Clyde E. Martin) was published in 1948, people worried that it would encourage a mechanical attitude toward sexual activity and thus give sex more of a scientific than a moral cast. Lionel Trilling expressed the concern at the time that "the tendency to divorce sex from other manifestations of life is already a strong one. This truly absorbing study of sex in charts and tables . . . may have the effect of strengthening the tendency still more with people who are by no means trained to invert the process of abstraction and to put the fact back into the general life from which it has been taken."

Yet Trilling himself must have known that such a fear was misplaced. America would not, cannot, disconnect sexual conduct from morality. Abortion, judged by many to be immoral in itself, compounds the felony of having sex at all. One reason abortion causes so deep a national disruption is because sex does, too. If

Americans could reproduce themselves by fission, they would probably do it.

~~~~

There may be one other reason for abortion's effect on the country in recent years, apart from our peculiar and peculiarly sensitive characteristics: Since the end of the Second World War, American society, not unlike modern Western societies in general, has shifted its intellectual basis from a humanistic to a social science culture—that is, from a culture used to dealing with contrarities to one that demands definite, provable answers. The rise of the social sciences in university curriculums since the early 1950s has not only had an enormous influence on the shape of higher education and on fields of endeavor (social work, education, psychology); it has influenced the way Americans as a whole think about their problems. Abortion may be thought about legitimately in a humanistic context or it may be considered in a social science context, but the contexts are vastly different and they lead to vastly different conclusions, attitudes, even moods.

The essential difference between the two is that social science leads to politics and humanism to more humanism. The nature and structure of social science thought is such that it tends not only to identify but to actually create issues that must be solved. Often these issues are most significant in terms of the country's progress. Civil rights, for example, was a subject that had to be understood as social science, however humanistic thought might have enforced the moral rightness of the issue, because without a political solution to the inequitable allocation of civil rights (i.e., the passage of laws), the subject would have floundered perpetually in public sorrow and head shaking, while those deprived of their civil rights would be deprived to this day.

Similarly, social science thinking has helped identify and crystallize problems of poverty, of the abuse of children, of education, and, frequently, problems related to work and family. It has helped empower groups that needed power. Every lobby in Washington is a direct descendant of a social science definition. It has affected language, creating categories or "types" of personality and situation, along with establishing various "syndromes." It has encouraged the feeling that every complaint can be a cause, a feeling that has produced both noble and stupid results.

What social science thinking does not encourage is human sympathy. I do not mean sentimental fellow feeling that acknowledges another's pain or discomfort; I mean the sort of intellectual sympathy that accepts another's views as both interesting and potentially valid, that deliberately goes to the heart of the thinking of the opposition and spends some time there. That sort of humanistic thinking may or may not be humane, but at least it offers the opportunity to arrive at a humane understanding outside the realm and rules of politics. In a way, it is a literary sort of thinking, gone now from a postliterary age, a "reading" of events to determine layers of depth, complication, and confusion.

The socially scientific mind regards complications as puzzles to be sorted out and does not readily admit confusion as a valuable intellectual element. Confusion leads to doubt, doubt to a changing of political position. To the humanistic mind, however, confusion is a positive tool of thought, whether or not it unravels itself or leads anywhere concrete. Confusion is the means by which one's comprehension is enlarged, even if it forces one to live in an enlarged muddle.

The modern refusal to live in an enlarged muddle existed before and outside the abortion debate, but when the debate arrived at center stage, it fit modern tendencies perfectly. Here was an issue that seemed to lend itself naturally to, indeed beg for, social science solutions: It involved human biology; it touched upon major professions and institutions; and it affected large numbers of people with opposing views. It also entailed making or remaking laws, thus it had widespread practical consequences. It had political consequences as well; people running for office would have to choose sides.

Everything that has happened in the abortion debate has been within the polarities that social science thinking creates. The quest to determine when life begins is a typical exercise of social science—the attempt to impose objective precision on a subjective area of speculation. Arguments over the mother's rights versus the rights of the unborn child are social science arguments, too. The social sciences are far more interested in rights than in how one arrives at what is right—that is both their strength and weakness. Thus the abortion debate has been political from the start.

A good many pro-choice advocates, in fact, came to lament the political character of the abortion debate when it first began. At that time, in the 1960s, political thinking in America was largely and conventionally liberal. The liberals had the numbers, therefore they felt they could set the national agenda without taking into account the valid feelings or objections of the conservative opposition. When in the presidential election of 1980 it became glaringly apparent that the feelings of the conservative opposition were not only valid but were in the political ascendancy, many liberals reconsidered the idea that abortion was purely a rights issue. They expressed appreciation of a more emotionally complicated attitude, one they realized they shared themselves, however they might vote. The confessional stories of pro-choice women who had had abortions but suffered real doubts and anguish were autobiographical expressions of humanistic thought, but by then the issue had gone too far to be returned to humanism.

If the abortion debate had risen in a humanistic intellectual environment, it might never have achieved the definition and clarity of the *Roe* v. *Wade* decision, yet it might have moved toward a greater consensus of thought among the public. One has to guess at such things through hindsight, of course. But in a world in which humanistic thought predominated, abortion might have been taken up in terms of its human elements, and the initial impulse in the debate might have gone toward discussing such unscientific and apolitical elements as human guilt, human choice, and human mystery.

That, as one sees now, is the opposite of what has happened. Instead of considering the human nature of the fetus, for instance, discussions (read shouting matches) have focused on the human *status* of the fetus—the fetus as legal entity. Much of the abortion debate has centered on the question of whether, as a person, the fetus has constitutional rights. The current trend to allow abortion rights to be decided on a state-by-state basis depends on how one defines the fetus. Some argue that the fetus is not a person, thus has no constitutional rights. Others argue that the fetus, as a person, must be protected by the individual states.

The illogic of the latter position was argued by the legal scholar Ronald Dworkin in the *New York Review of Books* when Dworkin pointed out that if the fetus does have constitutional rights as a person, then clearly it is entitled to equal protection under the law. If conversely the fetus has no constitutional status as a person, then no individual state may be permitted to interfere with the right of a mother, who *is* protected constitutionally, to terminate her pregnancy. That particular argument is merely one that continually occurs within the social sciences framework.

But what if one considered the fetus a person, even a person with full constitutional rights, and was still willing to terminate its existence, to kill it? That position would be very hard to hold, much less defend in a social sciences environment. Yet it is the kind of thinking that characterizes humanistic thought all the time. And it is in fact exactly the kind of thinking suggested by the polls—73 percent wanting abortion rights, 77 percent seeing abortion as murder. Instead of constructing a legalistic logic in which the fetus issue may be discussed, the humanist applies to it a moral logic. Suddenly, rights give way to nuances. Who has the right to live more? How does one know? Is it possible to believe in both contradictory rights simultaneously?

Questions like that are rare in modern American society and rarer still in the institutions of society that shape and control public conduct. Abortion as a modern issue has entered a society that seeks to be adamant and categorical about all issues, and to make them political. One might think that of all human problems, those pertaining to birth and to the termination of birth would give rise to the most complex, unsure, even the most beautiful sentiments and expressions of opinion. Instead, abortion has encouraged mere rage.

Yet if we could find the way to retrieve this kind of conflicted thinking, and find a way to apply it to the country's needs, we might be on our way toward a common understanding on abortion and perhaps toward a common good. Abortion requires us to think one way and another way simultaneously. Americans these days could make very good use of this bifurcated way of thinking.

Chapter 4

Life Itself

*T*o suggest that an approach acknowledging the ambivalent nature of abortion might lead the country toward a usable resolution brings me back to the concern voiced in Chapter 1: Americans are not speaking their true minds about abortion because their minds are in conflict. Yet living with conflict is normal in America, and our reluctance to do so openly in this matter, while understandable in an atmosphere of easy polarities, may help create a country in which we do not recognize ourselves. An America that declares abortion legal and says nothing more about it would be just as distorted as one that prohibited the practice. The ideal situation, in my view, would consist of a combination of laws, attitudes, and actions that would go toward satisfying both the rights of citizens and the doubts held by most of them.

Achieving this goal is, I believe, within reach. I know how odd that must sound when one considers the violent explosions that have occurred in places like Wichita as recently as August 1991, or when one sees the pro-life and pro-choice camps amassing ammunition for the 1992 presidential campaign. But for the ordinary private citizen, the elements of a reasonably satisfying resolution to the abortion problem are already in place. I keep returning to the fact that the great majority of Americans both favor abortion rights and disapprove of abortion. Were that conflict of thought to be openly expressed and were certain social remedies to derive from it, we would not find a middle of the road on this issue—logically, there is no middle of the road. But we might very well establish a wider road, which would accommodate a broad range of beliefs and opinions and allow us to move along.

What most Americans want to do with abortion is to permit it but discourage it also. Even those with the most pronounced political stands on the subject reveal this duality in the things they say; while making strong defenses of their positions, they nonetheless, if given time to work out their thoughts, allow for opposing views. Pro-choice advocates are often surprised to hear themselves speak of the immorality of taking a life. Pro-life people are surprised to hear themselves defend individual rights, especially women's rights. Both sides might be surprised to learn how similar are their visions of a society that makes abortion less necessary.

I discovered this by interviewing a number of people in

the state of Iowa during the gubernatorial and senatorial campaigns of the summer of 1990. My intention was to look at the state as a place to study the political issue, since abortion was a main factor that distinguished the candidates from one another in that election. As it turned out, Iowans proved less interesting on the politics of abortion than on their own divided thoughts.

No one state of the union is perfect for understanding a national issue, much less for offering a model of how that issue might be resolved, but Iowa has always been an especially good place for getting at the heart of what the country is thinking. Partly this is because the state seems to grow politics as easily as it grows feed corn; in most years, if the Iowa presidential caucuses did not already exist to frame the issues in the national contest, Iowans would invent a forum of their own. No matter that Ronald Reagan and George Bush were both defeated in recent caucuses. The state does not claim to be a bellwether of national opinion; it claims only to be sensible.

Iowa shows some remarkable statistics to verify its position as middle America. Geographically, the state is situated between the two great rivers of the continent, the Missouri and the Mississippi. It is bisected by the 42nd parallel, the symbol John Dos Passos used to locate classic American middleness; the 42nd parallel was the line followed by the transcontinental railroad and the transcontinental highway. Of the fifty states, Iowa ranks twenty-fifth in area and twenty-fifth in population. It ranks twenty-sixth in personal income. As if to emphasize its solidity, the state is divided into squares. Roads run either horizontally or vertically; there are no short cuts in Iowa.

Politically, Iowa's Democrats tend toward being Republicans, and its Republicans tend toward being Democrats. If there is a Republican governor, the state legislature is Democrat, and vice versa. The state is renowned for a dogged common sense attitude that approaches dullness (which it both mocks and enjoys), and it finds itself on the middle ground in almost everything. Seventy-five percent of all Iowans believe that flag burning should be made illegal as a form of political protest, which is a lot; but 83 percent of the country feels the same way. Few states can compete with Iowa either for unabashed patriotism or for the ardor of antiwar, antinuclear, and environmental movements.

Where the state rises from its middle ground is in such areas as literacy (Iowa ranks first as the nation's most literate state) and health. The state boasts the third lowest mortality rate, the tenth lowest disease rate, and ranks sixteenth highest in access to health care. Its homicide rate is low; it fell 31 percent, from 75 to 52, in 1989. This may be due to an aging population, since murder victims are usually young. Yet the incidence of felonies and misdemeanors is up since 1980, and the drug trade has infiltrated many of the small, innocent-seeming towns.

In the summer of 1990, when I was there, several drive-by shootings occurred in Des Moines, and a black man was shot by a white man in a Des Moines suburb in an incident that troubled the entire state. The black man was returning the white man's stolen wallet, which he had found. When the white man saw him standing in his doorway holding his wallet, he ran for his gun and shot him.

There was also a lot of talk that summer about Nancy Ziegenmeyer, in Grinnell. Ziegenmeyer had gained national notice earlier that year when she volunteered her name to the Des Moines *Register* after she had been raped. "Hundreds of women are raped and they all have to get up the next morning and get on with their lives and take care of their kids and families," said Sherry Thompson, a Grinnell factory worker. "They don't go on Donahue or do a book and make a fortune."

That attitude is characteristic of Iowans, who shun ostentation no matter how justified the circumstance. But equally characteristic is the desire to do right and to see right done, which makes Ziegenmeyer and Thompson Iowans alike. There is an insistent, almost irritating normality about the place, an apparently inborn desire to "get on with their lives." The attitude may come from traits inherited from the northern European immigrants who founded the state or simply from a people who know how hard it is to live off the land.

Jim Autry, a poet and recently retired editorial director of Meredith Publications in Des Moines, and his wife, Sally Pedersen, put it this way: "Farmers love and appreciate the land and they love and care for life," said Jim. "But they are utterly pragmatic about it. I mean, they raise things to kill." Sally added: "In the 4-H clubs young people raise a steer and groom that steer and care for it. And then they take it to the fair, win the blue or purple ribbon and they sell it and it gets slaughtered. And that is part of the reality of life."

The Autry-Pedersens, like most Iowans, have deep feelings for their state, which, again like most Iowans, they express with unsentimental affection and disinterested admiration. Jim says, "The driving force in this state is individualism, self-sufficient individualism. Take care of thyself and always be ready to take care of thy neighbor in need." He laughs. "I mean, don't *talk* to them. Just be ready to help." To illustrate the ethic, Jim and Sally alternate in singing lyrics from fellow Iowan Meredith Willson's *The Music Man:* "We can stand touching noses for a week at a time and never see eye to eye./But, what the heck! You're welcome,/Glad to have you with us." Don Avenson, the Democratic candidate for governor, also called upon Meredith Willson to define the state, and Marian Murphy, ninety-three, and her daughter Helen, who live in the west of the state in Red Oak, sang the same lyrics to make the same point.

"So here is this state of generally conservative people," says Jim, "people who should be defined as Republican conservatives in the classic sense of the term, who inevitably have great social programs, great education programs, great health care programs, and who will send a liberal to the Senate and Democrats to the state legislature to make sure they control it if a Republican is governor. There is always some common sense balance. They are never going to let one party run things, because one party is not to be trusted." That common sense balance seems to result in accommodations of thought on matters of friction as well.

The major theme struck by the interviews was a balance of individual independence and community needs. In the context of abortion, these two areas became another way of saying, permit but discourage—a formula by which the rights of the individual are preserved within the framework of the community and the other way round. Just as pro-life advocates often accuse their opponents of not caring about human life, pro-choice advocates accuse pro-life people of not caring about unwanted babies after they are born. In this, too, the interviews suggested otherwise. The most rabid pro-life advocates, no less than the pro-choice people, spoke unprodded of creating social remedies that would keep the need for abortion down.

Most of the people had had their fill of the subject by the time I brought it up to them yet one more time. Iowans had plenty of other things to occupy their minds that summer—the heat, for one thing. Sensible people kept indoors as much as possible, in air-conditioned cars and homes, while the white streets of the cities remained still and empty and the corn grew from "knee-high in July" to harvest in September and October. When people did emerge from the mechanically created cold, there were special summer events such as the Paul McCartney concert the day I arrived in July ("You here for the concert?") and the traditional Register's Annual Great Bike Race Across Iowa (RAGBRAI), sponsored by the Des Moines newspaper and the Indianola annual National Balloon Classic and Conrad's annual State Plowing Matches. At the Iowa State Fair the cow-chip toss was the subject of discussion and consternation. Seems that the more than two hundred cow chips had to be imported from neighboring Nebraska because fair officials were unable to find "clean, odor-free cow cookies" in Iowa.

As if to ensure that abortion was not entirely forgotten, about a hundred pro-choice and pro-life demonstrators gathered outside the Cedar Rapids Holiday Inn, where Supreme Court justice Sandra Day O'Connor was speaking at a banquet of the Herbert Hoover Presidential Library Association. O'Connor was confronted by pro-choice advocates, who staged a "die-in" by lying on the ground, to symbolize women who have died through self-induced abortions. Pro-life demonstrators gathered to protest the pro-choice demonstrators.

The subject was not likely to be forgotten in any case. There was the reality of the election, which saw pro-choice and Catholic Senator Tom Harkin, a Democrat, opposed by pro-life and Catholic Congressman Tom Tauke, a Republican, and the pro-life Republican Governor Terry Branstad and challenged by pro-choice Iowa House Speaker Don Avenson. Relevant things were happening in Iowa's neighboring states as well. Iowans realized that summer, as state after state all around them adopted more restrictive abortion laws, that they had achieved the curious position of being the only state in the region that looked the way *Roe* v. *Wade* intended the country to look.

Both by their temperament and by their situation, then, the people with whom I spoke, spoke for the country. By no means can Iowa be considered in the same light as New York or California, whose social problems are more diverse and severe and whose populations are a good deal more heterogeneous. Yet on the issue of abortion they covered the ground that citizens of any state would cover.

They also revealed those common areas of thought that could lead to the wider road I mentioned earlier, the place where we might recognize one another as citizens of the same country and sharers in the same problem, where we might simultaneously put abortion before and behind us.

Besides those already referred to, I spoke at length with about fifty Iowans, with some more than once, to try to get as many points of view as were available and to see if those views changed or evolved in a series of conversations.

Among those interviewed were John Crystal, the gubernatorial candidate who lost to Don Avenson in the Democratic primary; Mary Louise Smith, former chair of the National Republican party; David Yepsen, senior political writer for the *Des Moines Register* and his wife, Mary Stuart; Shelly Bain, executive director of NARAL in Iowa; Gerald (Pete) and Wineva Pedersen, Sally's parents, who live in the farm town of Vinton; Joe Rosenfield, a prominent retired businessman; Marlys Popma, president of the Iowa Right to Life Committee; Evelyn Davis, a black organizer and political activist in Des Moines; Flora and Frank Haker, an insurance salesman and his wife who live in the middle of the state; Robert Weir, a professor of medical ethics at the University of Iowa Medical School, in Iowa City; Jan Mickelson, a popular radio talk show host; Dr. Lee Van Voorhis of Sioux City, a physician who until recently had been the sole provider of abortions in the west of Iowa; pro-life leaders CeCe

Zenti and Mary Zmolek; Jerry Crawford, a former lawyer for Planned Parenthood; George Patterson, chaplain at the University of Iowa Hospital; Rita Swan, a child protection advocate in a small town in the west; Chris Roby, a postal worker; Minette Doderer, a longtime state representative, and several other state candidates, pro-life and pro-choice.

Of the two gubernatorial candidates, only Don Avenson made himself available to talk on the issue. The press office of Terry Branstad refused interviews repeatedly by failing to answer phone calls or by failing to respond when they said they would.

Every one of these people spoke with a personal concern about the subject, whether they happened to be pro-choice or pro-life, from the city or the country, young or old, married, parents, religious or not, Republican or Democrat or anything in between. By their thoughtfulness they demonstrated an undercurrent of great seriousness. Dr. Herbert Remer, who performs abortions in Des Moines, observed: "I don't think anyone takes [the subject] lightly. I think most women can tell you, years afterward, the exact date they had their abortions. They all take it very seriously. Women don't use abortion as birth control. That's a fantasy. We have statistics here. About 90 percent of women who have an abortion never have another one."

They also demonstrated by their responses many components of a national consensus on the subject, which, I am fairly certain, is ready to be expressed in public and converted into either a reaffirmation of *Roe* v. *Wade* or into a new law that makes the same guarantees. But their attitudes were also complicated. Most felt that abortion for mere convenience is morally wrong; that abortion is both a private affair and a community responsibility; that there is a moral presumption against taking a human life; that abortion constitutes some sort of killing act; that an absolute, prohibitive law on abortion is not enforceable, and that unenforceable laws are bad laws. However they came down on the issue politically, these were their feelings in common. Most often they were raised in the process of describing how they arrived at their political positions.

Almost all the pro-choice people, for instance, mentioned the qualms they had about abortion itself. Minette Doderer has been pro-choice consistently and is probably the most down-the-line liberal representative in the state legislature. She lives in Iowa City, in a modest house with more furniture than it needs. A small woman with short gray hair, Doderer's manner of speaking is brisk and matter-of-fact. At the outset she spoke forcefully of the importance of holding firm against the pro-life people. But then as she went on, she said, "You know, I don't like to think about [abortion]. Every once in a while it comes across my mind: Why am I doing this, defending abortion rights? Who likes to think of themselves killing a fetus? But then I think: I'm not the one making that decision. Another woman is doing it. And I don't think that anyone connected with a pregnant woman has the right to do anything but discuss it with her."

Rita Swan, who lives in Bronson (pop. 209), has a special view of the subject. Swan founded CHILD, Inc. to protect children from religious interference with their health. The Swans lost their sixteen-month-old son, Matthew, to bacterial meningitis, and they claim that the Christian Science Church, to which they once belonged, prevented the child from receiving treatment.

A sad and thoughtful woman with wide-set eyes, Swan, her husband, and their remaining child live in a small, isolated house overlooking a cornfield bisected by powerlines.

"I'm a pro-choice person," she said. "Politically, I think you have to maintain a choice for the woman. But I'm not opposed to the government regulating abortion to a certain extent. I would not be opposed to prohibiting abortions in the last trimester. I would not be opposed to requiring that fathers who are willing to support the children be allowed a voice in the decision making. I wouldn't be opposed to prohibiting abortions for sex selection. I'm willing to let the government regulate abortion, but I do think that there has to be some window of choice open for the woman. I just . . . I don't appreciate a lot of the pro-choice people's rhetoric. I think it's too strident and too simplistic. Gloria Steinem has said there's no difference between an abortion and a tonsillectomy, and I think that's a terrible thing to say. I think that's stupid. I don't like to see people denying that fetuses are living beings and I don't like to see them using subterfuge [issues] like pregnancy tissue, and I think the rhetoric has been real dishonest on both sides. And I wouldn't enjoy going out and making a public stance on it. I wouldn't enjoy going out and marching in a pro-choice march with a placard or whatever, because I do think it's an issue with competing claims that are both valid. I think the fetus is a human life and that abortion is murder of the innocent and the helpless, and I don't feel, you know, I don't feel comfortable with abortion. But I just think that prohibiting abortion would lead to severe degradation of women."

Evelyn Davis, a black activist in her sixties, lives and works with children in a black residential area of Des Moines. She is a large, matriarchial woman and is emphatically pro-choice. Yet she admits, "We want to be modern, but underneath I really have the feeling that it's unnecessary to get pregnant and not have the baby, because in my day a baby wasn't a burden no matter how old you were. I think that some people still have that in the back of their minds."

On the issue of viability, the gubernatorial candidate Don Avenson said that he is for the women's choice no matter how late the abortion. "Yet it affects me emotionally. I said the other day that I am willing to agree to abortions in the third trimester if a woman's life is involved. But it affects me emotionally."

It was interesting to me that very few of the people I spoke with were much concerned about the question of when life begins. Dr. Robert Weir, the ethics professor at the University of Iowa Medical School, has a professorial manner enhanced by a short beard and goggle-shaped wire-rim glasses. Dr. Weir has developed a highly structured definition of "personhood," dividing those he calls "potential persons" from others, but listening to him, one felt that his profession required him to draw those sorts of lines in an academic context. For the majority, there was general agreement that abortion involves the taking of a life at some stage, and that alone was grounds for serious thought. Yet it seemed typical of Iowans to quickly cut through an aspect of the subject that has both enchanted and confounded thinkers since the debate began.

Nor did they indicate that they believed that parental notification or parental consent offered a usable compromise on the issue. States surrounding Iowa have adopted parental notification laws either to simply make abortion more difficult or to attempt to create an attitude among citizens to see abortion as more of a familial or communal concern. But most of the Iowans I interviewed felt that their state was highly unlikely to pass parental notification laws, even though many people had some sympathy with the family-oriented aspirations of such laws.

"I think a lot of people who favor parental notification look at their own family unit and realize how hurtful that would be not to have notification available to them," said Mary Kramer, a pro-choice candidate for the state senate and an executive with Iowa Blue Cross/Blue Shield. Kramer talked in her office on the twenty-first floor of the Ruan Center, a business tower in Des Moines. A woman in her mid-fifties, she has a large, slightly babyish face, which, with her pink-tinted glasses, suggests a sense of play inside the businesswoman. On an easel in her office is the maxim "Every act of conscious learning requires the willingness to damage one's self-esteem."

"People favoring notification don't understand that the demographics of the family have changed radically. That if they have a nuclear family, father and mother and children, and father works and mother is at home, that not even 10 percent of the world is there anymore. Even in Iowa that's not 10 percent of the world. So when people ask me about notification, I say first of all you can't legislate the parent-child relationship, and that's what it's trying to do. And second of all, if this were a perfect world with wonderful families in place, notification wouldn't even be an issue.

"I work with the Young Woman Resource Center and the YWCA. You look at those programs and you see twelve-year-olds who have become pregnant and come from abusive situations. Now, what are my choices? I'm going to force that twelve-year-old to go through her pregnancy? And I'm going to force her to tell her abusive parents about it? What's just about that? And if you tell me that's true only in a small percentage of cases, then I'm going to tell you that one child is all it takes for me. One! So you can't get to me on the notification issue. It's not a perfect world. I have to help you see that families are not what you'd like them to be."

I asked Don Avenson why it would not be reasonable for a family to expect their daughter to come to them with so serious a problem. He was campaigning in Grinnell College, in Grinnell. He is a big man who often refers to his size in his speeches. That day he was dressed in a dark suit and spoke in a muted voice.

"I would expect my daughter to come to me if she were pregnant," he said. "But the fact of the matter is that 75 percent of the young women tell their parents already. Of the 25 percent that don't, 12.5 percent carry the fetus to term; you don't need approval for that. You don't need to tell your parents that you are pregnant and you're going to have a baby. Of the remaining 12.5 percent that don't tell their parents, usually most come from some kind of dysfunctional family, some setting that's terribly abusive and incestuous. They're frightened to death of telling anybody. Why would they go to court to do that? Of the small percentage that comes from functional families—I hope my daughter does too—you identify it. You say I certainly expect my daughter would talk with me. I have raised her to do that. I think we trust each other. But if she doesn't, I want her safe. I want her alive."

Even my pro-life respondents, while they felt that notification presented a political nose in the door for ending abortion altogether, did not think that Iowa would buy the idea. (Proposals have since been presented to the state legislature and have been defeated.) No one considered notification to be central to the basic argument. Typical of Iowans, they all focused on the basic, though not oversimplified, consideration of individual rights and community responsibilities.

Mary Kramer resented the "angry militancy" on both sides of the issue: "And where there is angry militancy, those are not the people who can provide a caring environment for the individual affected. In a way, it's the customer. I think about how we talk in the business world about who is the customer and how we should deal with the customer and what are the customer's needs. With abortion, who is the customer? Probably, a woman who has made a serious error in judgment. And what does she need? She has some choices to make before the system can determine what her needs are. The most commendable people on both sides are those who will counsel her through those choices, allowing her to make choices—before, during, after—whatever is best."

Kramer asked: "How will society cope with the pluralistic family situations we have now? That's what we ought to be worrying about. So that we don't have the bottom-line twelve-year-olds thinking, If I'm pregnant, I will have a baby and somebody will love me. The bigger issue, though, is what do we need to do as a society to prevent abortion from being the alternative."

One expects pro-choice advocates to argue for social remedies. Yet pro-life activist Mary Zmolek, of Iowans for Life, did not sound very different from Kramer. Zmolek, in her sixties and clearly in good physical shape, spoke in a room at the Iowans for L.I.F.E. (Life Is For Everyone) office that seemed to serve as a pro-life library: "I was very angry when Jesse Jackson came to Des Moines and got a standing ovation for the statement that pro-life people are only interested in the fetus. They don't give a damn about them after they are born. That's not true. I don't know a single person in pro-life who thinks that way."

Marlys Popma, president of the Iowa Right to Life Committee, fully supported this view. She is in her mid-thirties. In her cluttered office was a bulletin board covered with thank-you notes from students with whom she had visited and a huge picture of the Virgin Mary.

"First of all," said Popma, "I believe that if a young woman feels that she is capable of giving a good home for a child, then so be it. But everybody is starting to see the writing on the wall. The pro-life movement had better, doggone better, be ready to help in crisis pregnancies. To help, we are going to have to regear our focus. It is going to have to be geared toward dealing compassionately with that girl in crisis pregnancy. Am I going to be willing to take her child or her into my home and am I going to be willing, are we going to be willing in the Right To Life movement, to initiate and help in programs where these girls can continue their education? Where they don't necessarily have to get stuck on a welfare roll because they are children having children?"

Rita Swan broadened the issue and related it to her experience as a teacher: "I really do feel that it's a moral issue. I think that the fetus is a living being, I mean, you know, it's potential life. It's on a progression towards full-fledged human life and I think society should acknowledge what they're doing. Abortion is murder, and I think that the only way that I'm a pro-choice person is that unwanted pregnancies are an indictment of the whole society and they are a reflection of the fact that we are very irresponsible with our sexuality. We glamorize sex. We just see sex as a multimillion-dollar industry, and it's paraded before young people day and night as the way things are and the way things should be and, I mean, you just can hardly find a movie that doesn't show extramarital or premarital sex. I mean, our whole society is not taking adequate responsibility for children and for their own behavior and their own impact on others. And unwanted pregnancies are just one more facet of irresponsible, selfish, immature behavior, and I can't see that a twelve-year-old girl or a fifteen-year-old girl should have to bear all of the impact and the consequences of that. I mean, they're just too young. They haven't been given any guidance or direction or incentives to have a more responsible kind of behavior.

"One of my students, a freshman kid eighteen years old here in Iowa, blond Scandinavian guy, bright kid, walked up to me yesterday, and said, 'I have to be excused from class today. My girlfriend's in the hospital.' And I could see he was very upset, and I said, 'Well, what's the matter? You look very shaken. Is she sick?' And he said, 'Worse than that. She had a baby, and we didn't even know she was pregnant.' This is rural Iowa. I mean, this is not the ghettos of Chicago."

Mary Louise Smith, strongly pro-choice, did not sound much different from Marlys Popma. The former chairman of the Republican National Committee lives in a modern house in an elegant older section of Des Moines. Smith, a doctor's widow, has silver hair, bright blue eyes, and a long jaw. She seems to combine down-home common sense with intellectual aristocracy.

"The way to prevent abortion is to educate people how to avoid abortions. That's why I cannot understand why pro-lifers are against family planning. It seems to me that the strongest people on family planning ought to be those that are locked in against abortion. If it is such an evil, then what you ought to do is prevent it. And that argument—that we are compassionate about the poor, and about blacks and the other minorities, yet we encourage you to have your babies—does not carry through. There is no consistency without compassionate action after that baby is born.

"There's discrimination here, too. That is a very com-

pelling issue with me—the discrimination in public funding. I don't know how you can say even with *Roe* v. *Wade*
in place that abortion is anything but merely legal; if you
uphold the law, it's only okay for rich women. This bog-
gles my mind. It's clearly discriminatory. I mean, the
people who speak in terms of abortion, of upholding *Roe*
v. *Wade*, you know, or even those that don't talk about
Roe v. *Wade*, talk about abortion except in cases of
incest and rape, health of the mother, and then say but no
public funding. There is no way you can get those two
things to come together. Are you concerned only about
these things for wealthy women?"

The idea of discouraging the need for abortion through
social remedies, then, was one of the major areas of agreement among those interviewed. Obviously, to those who
are vehemently pro-life the most effective way to discourage abortion would be a law prohibiting it. Still, their
view of discouragement is extended to sex education,
improved health for the poor and postnatal care—areas
not usually associated with the pro-life point of view. If
the permit but discourage formula was to work in this
country, the discouragement aspect—I felt after these
interviews—would not be difficult for most people to
agree upon. Whether local, state, or federal government
would be inclined to aid in discouraging abortions
through concrete programs would be another matter.

Pro-life and pro-choice people also agreed on discouraging abortion by means of shoring up families and
raising society's values and moral behavior generally. In
this belief they were voicing a deep dissatisfaction with
America of the moment, a sense not only that the country

has lost its moral cohesion, which has long been a complaint of the times, but also that it is in danger of becoming something unrecognizable to its majority. So great an effort had been made in the direction of the exceptions to society's norms, they felt, that the norms were about to be abandoned.

Some people, like pro-life advocate Jan Mickelson, drew odd connections between abortion and other signs of social disintegration. Mickelson, an overbearing, bearded man in his early forties, is a talk show host on WHO radio. He speaks with a resonant radio voice:

"I say that abortion is never okay, under any circumstances, because of what it does to the people having them and to the society at large that permits them. It's the same thing as the insensitivity that allowed the S & L situation to happen. It's the same insensitivity that allows Andrew Dice Clay to be popular. It's the same insensitivity that allows 2 Live Crew. A society that permits us to be dropped to the lowest common denominator is not going to be a very pleasant place to live. We will have lost the quality of our life, and to a great degree, mainstream normal, moral taxpaying citizens feel fatigued, tired of paying other people's bills and watching the cherished institutions that they love being debased day in and day out. Abortion is just one of the players in that culture war that we are talking about. And most of the troops are tired. They want to go home.

"What of the next generation?" asked Mickelson. "Economically, they'll be less safe in the streets, their lives and livelihoods will have less to look forward to. They'll live in a thoroughly debased culture that can't protect the flag, that considers a urine-soaked flag art work. And a guy with a bullwhip up his butt considered tax-supported art expression. I mean, that's bizarre. That is really bizarre. And it has to do with the moral collapse and the lack of thinking and stamina of the leadership of a generation. I can't sit back and be nonpartisan when I see what is happening to a country that I love and the people that I love. Now, how to rebuild that so people, so women, so relationships, don't ever feel that abortion is a necessity, that's the big challenge."

Jerry Crawford, though he was a lawyer for Planned Parenthood, had the same point of view. Over breakfast in the Des Moines Marriott Hotel, the forty-one-year-old attorney said: "You know, my pro-choice friends talk about crack-addicted babies or unwanted children or AIDS babies. What's the point? We have abortion on demand. What is the argument here? That we have X number of those kind of babies now and that if we didn't have abortion on demand, we'd have more of them? Is that the point? I'm not sure. What I am sure of is that until we restrict abortion on demand, people will not focus where I think as moral teachers we should focus, which is on education, prevention, and contraception. There's no incentive today for your thirteen-year-old in the ghetto to act responsibly when it comes to her sexuality because she knows she can have an abortion. There's *absolutely* no incentive, and if you could get them to tell you the truth, they would tell you at Planned Parenthood here and everywhere else in America and the other abortion clinics, people come back a second, a third, a fourth, and a fifth time. I mean, it's just pure irresponsible birth control." Dr. Remer's experience contradicted this contention.

Except for the specific question of allowing or not allowing abortion, the respondents saw society's collapse in much the same ways. For both sides the high number of abortions was a symptom of that collapse. It was time to return to or re-create an America, or at least an Iowa that they knew. This was not to be a country of moralistic posing but of values realized in community help. Thus, they said, would abortion be discouraged.

The "permit" part of the formula would offer much more of a problem for the pro-life side. Several pro-life supporters with whom I spoke reluctantly allowed for the exceptions of rape, incest, and the threat to the mother's life, but many of them did not and none indicated that there were any grounds for compromising their basic stand. I did not see how there could be. As I suggested in Chapter 1, if abortion is considered murder, it can never be entirely acceptable to those who oppose it, and if they are absolute in their opposition, they could never logically favor a system in which the practice was permitted.

Favoring a system is different from being willing to live with it, however. Just as there are millions of Americans who oppose capital punishment yet reside in a state where it is the law, the idea of a sort of loyal opposition of pro-life advocates living in a pro-choice country is not out of the question. Within the discussion of permitting abortion there may be other related grounds for conciliation. And people who oppose one another on the narrow issue may recognize shared values on some wider ones.

In my interviews, one of those shared values was privacy. The pro-choice people, as one would expect, extolled privacy as the basis for their position. Yet the pro-life people showed an equal reverence for private values and individual rights. Of course, those who were against abortion under any conditions were not about to extend their respect for private values to a forfeit of their position. And it would be a stretch to assume that simply because one appreciates the value of privacy and individual rights one is ready to be persuaded by the pro-choice argument. All that the expressions of respect for privacy did on both sides was to expose a potential ground for discussion. Yet for that alone it seemed significant.

One of the interesting things about the subject of abortion, unlike most divisive issues, is that opinions on it are usually founded in private values. I do not mean that they necessarily derive from the personal experience of having an abortion, but they often arise out of such personal elements as one's love of family or childhood memories, good and bad, or an individual sense of wonder at the process of birth or at genetics; or they arise from the course of one's individual fate. People do not speak of abortion the way they speak of war, taxes, or even the environment. They are often inconsistent in what they say. And they acknowledge their inconsistencies without apologizing for them, which suggests both how much of their thinking comes from the heart and how much they trust the heart's peculiar forms of reasoning.

Flora Haker, a woman in her thirties who deeply regrets the abortion she had at the age of nineteen, spends her free time working for the pro-life movement in middle rural Iowa. So does her husband, Frank, who sells insurance. They talked to me in a park in Vinton, a town of five thousand about a hundred miles north of Des Moines. Flora wore silver nail polish. Frank, who was dressed in blue sweatpants and a white sweatshirt, sat beside his wife. Behind them in the early evening was a deserted playground and, in the distance, a water tower shaped like a mushroom cloud.

After two hours of articulating her position and noting its basis in personal guilt, Flora finally said that what she would really prefer is a system in which abortion is possible but not officially condoned. "If a girl really wants an abortion and she's had a lot of counseling and has been presented with all the facts and she is still determined, I'd rather see her get a safe abortion by a doctor than find someone who'd do it illegally."

Many others with whom I spoke went through similar shifts of thought and modifications of position. They did so not because they doubted their stand on the issue but because the subject, if it is to be confronted honestly, almost demands certain inconsistencies on both sides. I felt frequently that the people I interviewed were aware of their inconsistencies for the first time when they expressed them aloud—something they rarely did, given the confrontational atmosphere in which the subject exists. One of the virtues of making private values public, even in a single interview, was to see how complicated and fluid they could be.

Jerry Crawford, the former Planned Parenthood lawyer, recalled being visited by an administrator of the organization, who put the question to him flatly: "What is *your* position on abortion?"

"I remember sort of being overcome with a feeling of inadequately being able to respond to the question because I wasn't able to say, 'I'm for it' or 'I'm against it' the way so many people seem to find it so easy to do. I'm still not able to say I'm for it or I'm against it. I wish my mind worked that way sometimes, the way it does seem to for so many people, but it doesn't. And I wasn't able to answer her question, and I remember thinking out loud sort of with her and saying that I was very bothered about a constitutional approach that said if you had money, you could have an abortion, but if you didn't you couldn't. That struck at something I thought . . . I thought that was fundamentally wrong and fundamentally violative of my feelings about equal protection and about equality in general and about economic justice, and yet I was also very aware that I was not a proponent for abortion on demand, at the same time."

The University of Iowa chaplain, George Patterson, spoke of a similar balancing act. Patterson sat at one end of a couch in his office. His desk was piled high with books. He is a pale, boyish-looking man in his fifties. His reading glasses rested in his lap.

"Well, this goes back to about the late 1960s, when I had always assumed that abortion was illegal and therefore morally wrong, except in extraordinary cases to preserve the life of a mother. But the debate was beginning. And I suppose by the time of the early seventies, before *Roe* v. *Wade*, I was one of those who was hoping there would be some kind of decision to open up. At that time I was pretty much pro-choice and for a number of years afterwards. Something impacted my thinking the last three or four years. When I began to think about the fact that pro-life people who demonstrate so noisily and so disturbingly in public are doing some of the same things that I was doing when I demonstrated against the war in Vietnam in the late sixties and early seventies. So I have to respect their convictions, even if I don't agree with them.

"My thinking about this, I guess, is I think abortion has to be available legally as a choice for women. I think the best law is a permissive law. On the other hand, I hope that women will use it sparingly, make it the last resort instead of the first resort. That's not because I believe that personality begins at conception. Does life begin at conception? Sure. Is it human life? Yes, it's human life. Is it the life of a person? That's a different question. I'm not willing to come down to that. But within Christianity there is a long tradition that life deserves the most protection when it is most vulnerable. And for that reason, I think then the decision to terminate a pregnancy is a grave moral decision, you know. But I'm not saying it shouldn't be made at some times. I'm not saying that there aren't times when I could support that decision."

Then Patterson said something that pointed to part of a resolution: "We have to live and get along with people who disagree with us on some fundamental things. It seems to me one of the ways we have done this is to make increasing various kinds of decisions sort of private. You know, I have my beliefs, you have your beliefs. Certainly, religion is that way. That's the way we get along with each other religiously. We decide this is a very personal matter and for the most part we don't argue in public debate. And I think that belongs to things like sexual morality and abortion."

Patterson's formulation, it seemed to me, opened the way for a good many pro-life people to tolerate a pro-choice law. Of course, that would depend on one's respect for privacy superseding one's opposition to abortion. And even in pro-choice minds, private values are not absolute.

Jim Autry and Sally Pedersen live in a handsome house in Des Moines, not far from Mary Louise Smith. Jim, originally from Mississippi, speaks in a soft Southern dialect and looks twenty years younger than his age, sixty. Sally is a tall, striking woman with a strong, intelligent face. They have an autistic child, Ronald, whose difficulties are more than offset by his intellectual curiosity and affectionate nature. After dinner at home, Jim and Sally told of the premature birth of their friends' twins, one of whom, the boy, died. Yet the girl, born at under two pounds, survived. Jim said:

"I'm really stunned by that—not just the tragedy of it, but by the miracle of it as well. I remember seeing Sarah, I remember looking at her and thinking. This baby can't live. We've got to get ready for another funeral, here. I remember thinking that over and over and over again. And here she is a healthy-looking little kid holding her head up and gurgling and being a little baby. And it gives me a lot of qualms about this issue. One could put forth contention that medical technology can preserve this life.

Whose decision is it then? Is it the woman's choice because this life happens to be in her body? Well, I believe that. Up to what point do I believe that? Is it personhood? Is it a question of soul? Is it a question of God's creature? What is the question? I don't have the answer to it. But I think at some point the question is going to have to turn on the viability of the life by everything we know and are able to do."

I asked him why is that, if viability is dependent on the advancement of medical technology. Why should one's position on choice be any difference in principle if the baby is viable after two months or two days?

Sally and Jim then got into this exchange:

JIM: I don't know. If the baby can come out of the mother's body and live and grow, then I think that throws a little different aspect into the question. If you can pull them out and put them in a test tube and let them grow, well, then abortion is no big deal anymore.

SALLY: But I guess in my mind, and obviously you know I don't see this the same way as you're seeing it, but I feel that Sarah's parents had the right to make the decision *not* to use all this technology.

JIM: But they couldn't have made the decision not to use any of it. There's a certain minimum technology.

SALLY: Right. But there are those people who are making those choices and I think that is okay. And I guess I don't think we ought to sit in judgment on one another . . .

JIM: . . . No, I agree. I agree . . .

SALLY: . . . because you are choosing to make a child that

you are going to raise and care for. And it's going to be part of your family for the rest of your life. It's not like you're producing something for society.

Sally's argument would not prevail among staunch pro-life advocates, but the idea that one's personal beliefs are at the center of the moral question appealed to both sides. It seemed clear from these interviews that Iowans had an extraordinary appreciation of their right to think and act as free individuals and that the appeal of the pro-choice movement to the majority was as much a part of that appreciation as it was based on the movement's own merits. For their part, the pro-life people had an especially hard time arguing against individual rights even as they advocated laws that would impose on or modify those rights. Often, those most strongly pro-life were also those who had opposed Iowa's seat-belt law on the grounds that the law restricted individual choice.

The value of privacy, in other words, meant at least as much to the pro-life people as the value of life, the two being bound to each other. One could read this conflict of values in their responses to questions and in their gestures, glances, and intonations as well.

Some pro-life people had worked out their conflict in favor of community responsibility on the abortion issue specifically and perhaps exclusively.

Chris Roby, a postal worker in her late thirties with prematurely gray hair, sat in Perkins, "a family restaurant" in Des Moines. She talked of abortion as "something people should protect each other from."

Flora Haker compared abortion to slavery: "Basically, I'm a conservative, and I believe that we stay out of other people's lives unless they're hurting somebody. Then I think we have an obligation as a society to protect those that are being hurt. You know, just as in the 1860s we had the obligation to society. The blacks were being treated like animals. That divided our country on that, and the slaveowners really felt that it was their right to own them, that [slaves were] their property. And I see abortion as very similar. We had as a society an obligation to see that these people had freedom just as we have it. And yes, there was going to be bloodshed over it because the slave-owners were being told to give up their property. But the blacks were people. We made choices then too."

Yet many more pro-choice people had worked out the conflict in favor of what Jim Autry termed Iowa's "self-sufficient individualism" even when they said that they would not have abortions themselves and might counsel others away from it.

Where private values were most severely tested was on the question of free will versus God's will or design. In defending the practice of birth control, while at the same time holding his pro-life position, Jan Mickelson said that "birth control presumes human sovereignty. But human beings aren't sovereign all the time. I don't know if I'm being coherent here or not, but my belief is that life is sacred, that all of human life is a reflection of God's character in His moral universe." If birth control happens to work, he said, then human control over procreation is part of God's plan. When it doesn't work, that is part of God's plan, too. Thus free will is only free within a divine framework. Mary Zmolek, of Iowans for L.I.F.E., said that "pro-life begins in a belief in God."

George Patterson took a different view. "Life is a gift of God," said the chaplain. "I believe that very strongly. But conception of the child is not a result of direct intervention. It is a human act between two people. We have to accept responsibility for that. And there may be times when responsibility involves terminating pregnancy."

This is exactly the sort of argument that makes Mary Louise Smith feel the entire abortion issue should be understood as a matter of freedom of religion:

"There is so much rhetoric now among the people that debate this, and particularly those that are advocating the pro-life side, and I see their banners and their posters and stuff at rallies, you know. And there is a lot about how it's a crime to kill, and murderers, and godlessness. They insert that. That clearly enters the debate, the religious aspect of it. My religion doesn't teach that. I'm a Protestant, United Church of Christ Congregational. My religion does not teach abortion is murder. So if indeed it is a religious issue, then to me that argues for leaving the thing alone entirely."

"If there's anything that bothers me," said John Crystal, a former gubernatorial candidate, "it's people trying to force their judgments on someone else. And that's what this is—a right-to-privacy issue. The right of people to have their own personal and religious beliefs."

Wineva (Winnie) Pedersen, Sally's mother, has worked out her own compromise. She and her husband, Gerald, called Pete, live in a Victorian house in Vinton.

Pete is tall and tanned and has a surprised look when he talks. Winnie has an alert face with small features.

"Well, you just can't fight Mother Nature," she said. "I spent a year or so in the South during World War II, and they were more laid back and didn't worry about tomorrow. But when you come to Iowa, it really is important to get the planting done and the work done when the sun's shining, because we know it doesn't shine every day and it does snow, and so I really think we just are governed by nature. And that's a wonderful connection because acceptance of nature is almost the same as the acceptance of God."

I suggested that a pro-life advocate might say, "That's just the reason that I'm against abortion. Birth under any circumstance is my acceptance of nature and God."

"I can't explain all my feelings," said Winnie, "except that I also have a problem, question, about how and where and how much medicine gets into this. If doctors and medical science are a tool of God, then that's one of the tools that God gave them. So I'm not sure that that's a good answer. But if we're going to have science, since we *do* have science, then there must be good places to use it. Some of the places we're using it aren't so good. Perpetuating life way beyond its years, I'm not sure about that. But we're dabbling with life there, so isn't this the same thing? If it's all right to extend life, why don't we have some control in the beginning? That balances to me."

And Patterson suggested there is no necessary collision between religion and private values: "Life that is most vulnerable deserves our greatest protection. That applies not only to the life of the fetus but to the life of the pregnant woman. I don't think [religion] gives us any clear and specific guidance on Thou shall not sin. And for that reason I think we have to respect the right of the individual conscience. I think that's all we can do. I think as clergy, it's our responsibility to help the individual think through the issue. If we're counseled to think the issue through as clearly as possible and to be sure the decision they're contemplating is one they can live with, not only practically and psychologically but morally and spiritually. But it really does represent their deepest convictions. And I think we have to let them make the choice and stand by it, whichever way it goes."

There was another issue, connected to privacy, on which most of the pro-life and pro-choice advocates also readily agreed: that the abortion conflict was in many respects a battle between men and women and that men on both sides of the question were interfering with a woman's problems and prerogatives.

Shelly Bain, the executive director of NARAL, spoke in her Des Moines office. A practiced debater on the subject, she often talked in complete paragraphs.

Bain saw the whole question of abortion as a man-woman issue: Men make the laws and women are forced to obey them. The men who are pro-life, according to Bain, are simply exercising their power over women, telling women what they may or may not do with their bodies. The women in the pro-life movement, she said, are merely fulfilling their traditional role of subjugation. "Women are the only ones who are going to get pregnant and have to deal with this issue."

I asked her if abortion was in any way a man's issue too.

"Yeah, it's for men who recognize the autonomy of women, who love women. Not for what women do for them—they are my wife or my mother—but who recognize that women are human beings and have a right to exist on their own, not as an appendage to them or as a helpmate."

Few of the people I interviewed took as extreme a view as Bain's, but as she was the first person with whom I spoke, I decided to put her theory to everyone else as I went along. Almost every woman and most of the men agreed with her.

Joe Rosenfield, a prominent Iowa businessman, and John Crystal both agreed. Rosenfield and Crystal, both elderly bachelors, live together in a modern apartment with large picture windows in Des Moines. Crystal said: "The church, by and large, teaches the inequality of women and men." Rosenfield added: "One thing is for sure—women are more intense in their feelings about [abortion]." For that reason, and because women also have the numbers on their side, Rosenfield also said that they would have more power as voters both in Iowa's elections and the presidential elections of 1992. "Men will vote for a candidate even if they disagree with his abortion position. Women will not."

Minette Doderer may have surprised herself in revealing how intense were her feelings: "There's no operation a male has that he's got to get government permission for." Doderer believes that male domination is so ingrained in the culture that it is often demonstrated unconsciously:

172 · Roger Rosenblatt

"I know one young man who is a dear friend, we're very close. He came from this district. When he was in the House, he was not really a practicing Catholic, but he had grown up in the Church and always liked to think he was a Catholic. And he was voting against a bill that the House had up, not one that had ever got to the Senate. And I said, 'Why are you going with that?' And he said, 'But I'm Catholic, Minette. That's the way I've always been taught. It's a sin.' I said, 'Were you ever in danger of impregnating any woman besides your wife?' He said, 'Well, yeah.' He admitted he played around in his day. And I said, 'You were just going to abandon them? Or were you going to divorce your wife and marry them to have the child?' Of course he wouldn't! You know, he got all flustered. He never thought of it. Or he never connected it with the sex act, I guess is what I'm saying, this baby. And he turned around and he voted the other way. And I asked him—he came over and he was real proud of his vote—I said, 'Why did you do that?' And he said, 'You got to me.'"

She also spoke of the responsibility that ought to be shared by men and women, but is not:

"A whole bunch of people think it's the woman's own fault. You know, she should have said no. She shouldn't have gotten herself pregnant. I have yet to hear anyone say, 'He should not have had sex with her.' Have you ever heard anyone say that? Have you ever heard them say the man should have said no, or ever read it or that's the solution? It's a woman's problem."

Sally Pedersen believes that much of the opposition to abortion was spurred by the increasing independence of

women in the 1960s—specifically, by the feminist movement and the introduction of the pill. To make her view
clear, she offered, semi-seriously, the following proposition:

"When young men move into puberty you tie their
testicles so there is not viable sperm. Then when they
have a relationship with a woman and they are ready to
have a child, the woman signs a consent form and they
reverse the procedures and the male is able to impregnate
a woman. Now, this does not do anything to his masculin-
ity, but do you think that idea would be well received?
You know, people would be outraged at such a thought.
But the only reason they would be outraged is because it
involves control over the male's reproductivity. Yet we
say to women, you know, whatever the circumstances are:
You are going to deliver this baby. Do you know what
carrying a pregnancy is and what the delivery is? If men
were made to go through that against their will, it would
not be done. I'm talking about a minor procedure that
would simply alleviate unwanted pregnancy and we
wouldn't have to worry about killing babies. Who would
buy that?"

On the pro-life side, Flora Haker was equally vehement
about the subservient role of women and the attacks on
a woman's independence. She said outright: "I don't
think that any man should be involved in the pro-life
movement." Her husband, Frank, looked uneasy. And
Cece Zente and Marlys Popma also spoke of the special
interests and responsibilities of women versus men, in the
act of giving birth and in the functions of parenthood.
Pro-choice supporters felt that women have the right to

choose. Pro-life supporters felt that women have the obligation not to choose. Both focused on a woman's private thought processes and values.

As noted earlier, the fact that the majority of my pro-life respondents embraced the validity of individual opinion did not mean that they were about to go over to the pro-choice camp. All it suggested was that there was an area of common thought in which they might recognize the basis of the pro-choice stand. Similarly, the fact that pro-life people, contrary to their reputation, supported social efforts to deal with unwanted pregnancies and unwanted children was not going to persuade pro-choice advocates to give up their ground. Here, too, an area of potential mutual understanding was disclosed.

The revelation of such areas in complicated matters of conflict, however, is no small thing in a democracy. There are issues Americans confront every day that will never be, can never be, resolved to everyone's satisfaction, yet the ability of one side to see the other with a certain degree of intellectual or emotional sympathy makes the issue tolerable and prevents it from becoming an exploding mine every time someone touches it. The majority rule ingredient of a democracy is clear. But the minority has the right to expect that its position, if at all sensible, will be appreciated and, where it is practicable, even taken into account.

In the conflict offered by abortion there is one solution that can be accepted by everybody and one that cannot. Pro-life and pro-choice advocates can join forces in working to discourage abortion without any strain to their philosophies. Logically, that cannot happen with regard to permitting abortion. Still, those who do not wish to see abortions permitted are a distinct minority, and they bear a responsibility toward the country and its form of government to behave like a minority—that is, to oppose the majority without destroying the country until or unless their position eventually prevails. That stance may be easier to accept if they concentrate on the respect for private values that they share with their opponents.

It is to say that both sides have strong interests in individuality and community, the interests characteristic of Iowans, and that both have reasonable attitudes on how individuality and community can be defined and served. Many more Americans see abortion as a necessary option for the country than as "something people should protect each other from," thus, I believe, that view ought to hold. But there is a great deal of room, certainly more than has been made apparent, for allowing abortion to become one of the normal conflicts of the country and not to remain the incendiary item it is at the moment. Iowans, said Mary Louise Smith, learn their moderation by being closer to the "natural progression of things." The natural progression of this subject may lie in identifying its areas of agreement and disagreement and in discovering that there is at least as much consensus as discord.

As Iowa goes, so might go the country. Iowa is likely to be pro-choice always, but pro-choice with the sort of reservations that humanize the issue and make the practice of abortion more palatable all around. It should be evident from the responses of the people I interviewed that they all—pro-choice and pro-life alike—look upon the killing element of abortion with appropriate gravity.

It is that gravity, as much as the particular opinion of one side or the other, that would allow the permit but discourage formula to be acceptable to most Americans.

If one combines the sense of social responsibility with the advocacy of individual rights expressed by these people, the resolution of permit but discourage seems within reach. The discouragement part is the easier to find agreement on, but when one looks upon the permission question as existing within a respect for private values, even that may become more acceptable. Remember again that already 73 percent of America finds abortion acceptable. Even more people may find it so if they can tolerate living in a country in which they may exercise the individual right not to have an abortion themselves or to argue against others having one yet still go along with the majority, who want the practice continued.

The question may be one of emphasis. Pro-life advocates would not be the losers in the battle if the end result should be to permit but discourage; they would merely be acting on their moral choice without interfering with others'. Some may judge such interference as the necessary adjunct to their moral position, but others may learn to satisfy their individual morality simply by holding on to it. All Iowans are by temperament pro-choice because they stress the freedom of the individual. And they are temperamentally pro-life by realizing the role of the community in individual welfare.

Iowa may not be the ideal state in everything, but in this debate it seems to me to have the golden mean before it and within it. Not only does an attitude of permit but discourage allow a people to live with ambivalence; it certifies the value of the American individual while at the same time pointing to the improvement of the group, of society as a whole. After the summer I spent in Iowa, I came away feeling that Iowans held a secret that, once revealed, could do everyone considerable good.

Were this balance of thought and attitude to be spoken aloud, it might serve some of the country's wider purposes as well, especially now when there is so much anguish over how we have lost our national identity and character. The character we lost, it seems to me, was one that exalted the individual in terms of what the individual did for the community. It honored and embodied both privacy and selflessness. A balanced attitude on abortion would also do both. It would make a splendid irony if this most painful and troublesome issue could be converted into a building block for a renewed national pride based in good will.

For that to happen the leadership of the country has to express itself as well, and Mario Cuomo excepted, that has not happened. Even Cuomo has spoken more in defense of his own personal ambivalence than as a leader urging the benefits of ambivalence on his countrymen. Both presidents Reagan and Bush have, I believe, done the issue and the nation much harm in not saying something like permit but discourage. By striking the pro-life pose, they have cannily appealed to a certain constituency without damaging their standing with the majority. But why could they not speak for the majority and still retain their principles by at once noting the necessity of abortion and deploring it?

As for Congress, it hardly seems too much to expect

our representatives to say something representative about the issue. Should *Roe* v. *Wade* be overturned, as may well happen, the country could be blown apart. To leave the matter to the states, as I have suggested earlier, would lead to mayhem. Congress used to pass laws, remember? I think it is time for Congress to make a law like *Roe* v. *Wade* that fully protects abortion rights but legislates the kind of community help like sex education that would diminish the practice.

To take a stand against abortion while also allowing for its existence can turn out to be a progressive philosophy. It both speaks for moral seriousness and moves in the direction of ameliorating conditions of ignorance, poverty, the social self-destruction of fragmented families, and the loss of spiritual values in general. The improvements of our lot that might begin with the impulse to decrease abortion might grow much wider, extending to the creation of a new, more generous, and productive American community, which has long been sought. What started as a debate as to when life begins might lead to making life better.

At the outset of this discussion I said that most Americans know how they feel about abortion, and if we would say so explicitly and frequently and with all our conflicts on the table, a resolution to this crisis might be possible. At least a resolution to the *feeling* of crisis, the emotions that create an atmosphere of relentless unreasoning hate might be possible. For the issue itself to be settled, of course, would require so dramatic and permanent a change in national attitudes toward sex, health, family values, and the poor that abortion would be eradicated by being rendered obsolete.

As unlikely an eventuality as that is, it is not out of the question for us to turn a negative element in our lives into an instrument for good. I believe that the permit but discourage attitude on abortion, as evidenced in Iowa, is ready to surface. Once it does, I hope that *Roe* v. *Wade* remains intact or that Congress passes a law that expresses the same stipulations. But should *Roe* be retained or if there should be a new law, it would be heartening to see wording attached that conveyed the range and complexity of feelings on the issue, that acknowledged that abortion is the taking of life at some stage, and that voiced the concern of the country that the best antidote to abortion is to make it less necessary. It is right that we have the choice, but it would be better if we did not have to make it.

The effort to reduce the necessity of abortion, which is the same as an effort to improve much that needs improving in this country, is to choose life as wholeheartedly as it is to be "pro-life." By such an effort one is choosing life for millions who do not want to be, who do not deserve to be, forever hobbled by an accident, a mistake, or by miseducation. By such an effort one is also choosing a different sort of life for the country as a whole—a more sympathetic life in which we acknowledge, privileged and unprivileged alike, that we have the same doubts and mysteries and hopes for one another.

In Chapter 3 I noted America's obsessive moral character, our impassioned tendency to treat every moral question that comes before us as a test of our national soul. That tendency is not so bad, however, if we happen to pass the test. The permit but discourage formula on abortion offers the chance to test our national soul by appealing to its basic egalitarian impulse. Were we once again to work actively toward creating a country where everyone had the same health care, the same sex education, the same opportunity for economic survival, the same sense of personal dignity and worth, we would see both fewer abortions and a more respectable America.

All those elements of national friction—individualism, optimism, the presence of evil, the fear of sexuality— might also find a positive context. The permit but discourage formula satisfies both the self-serving and the community-serving aspects of American individualism. It appeals to the retrospective side as well in urging a return to family and spiritual values. The forward-looking nature of the formula helps remove the abortion debate from the question of evil. And it could relieve us from the puritanical view of sex without undermining our middle-class stabilities.

Those caricatures I drew at the beginning of this book: Picture the two combatants laying down their signs and slogans and staring at each other with sympathetic curiosity. They begin to ask questions of each other. They listen to the answers. Slowly, awkwardly, they detect grounds of agreement. They occupy those grounds. From time to time they argue, and often they gaze separately into the distance with an imponderable helplessness. Yet they do not quit each other's company. And eventually they touch, surprised to discover that they were always within reach.

This too is the American dream, as possible as it is impossible, and as near as the life we share.

A Note on Opinion Polls

Figures represent findings of Louis Harris and Associates, Inc. and the Gallup Organization, computed within a year of each other. Additional polls are noted.

The following was asked by Harris in an independent poll in June 1990: "Do you favor or oppose giving a woman, with the advice of her physician, the right to choose to have an abortion?" Seventy-three percent responded in favor of that right.

In February 1991, Gallup, in a poll sponsored by Americans United for Life, asked: "Which of these statements best describes your feelings about abortion?" The response was as follows: 36.8 percent said that "Abortion is Just as Bad as Killing a Person Who has already Been Born, it is Murder;" 11.5 percent said that "Abortion is Murder, but it is Not as Bad as Killing Someone Who has Already Been Born;" 28.3 percent said: "Abortion is Not Murder, but it does involve the Taking of Human Life."

In its executive summary, Americans United for Life present these figures under the heading "Is Abortion the Taking of a Human Life?" They then write: "Seventy-seven percent of the respondents believe abortion is either an act of murder as bad as killing a born human being (37%), an act of murder, but not as bad as killing a born human being (12%), or the taking of a human life (28%)."

Please note how the statement was posed and then how it was qualified. The final 28 percent was grouped with those who consider abortion an act of murder, though in fact they were responding to a statement that referred to abortion not as murder but as the "Taking of Human Life." Also note in the above questions which words are capitalized: *Abortion, Just, Bad, Killing, Person, Who, Murder, Taking, Human*, and *Life.*

By being introduced with a headline that relates to abortion as the "Taking of a Human Life," the figure of 77 percent is legitimized to include all the responses. However, it is then quantified under the classification of murder, thus promoting the sense that this percentage actually deems abortion as murder.

In reality, only 49 percent agreed that abortion was murder, a figure more consistent with earlier polls. In an independent poll conducted in January 1985, Harris presented this statement: "To perform an abortion, even during the first three months of pregnancy, is the equivalent of murder because the fetus's life has been eliminated."

Fifty-two percent agreed; 44 percent disagreed. The same statement presented in 1981 received this response: 49 percent agreed; 47 percent disagreed. I use the highest figure (77 percent) because I can make no significant distinction between murder and the taking of a life. Because others can, however, I use the term *a form of murder.*

Eighty-two percent responded that abortion should be legal

(32 percent said always legal; 50 percent said legal depending on circumstances.)

In a 1980 poll, researchers for *The New York Times*/CBS News Poll asked whether there should be a constitutional amendment prohibiting abortion, and only 29 percent of respondents favored such an amendment. But when the same people were asked if there should be a constitutional amendment protecting the life of the unborn child, 50 percent said they would favor one.

According to *New York Times*/CBS polls on abortion conducted regularly since 1980, consistently about 61 percent respond favorably to the question: "If a woman wants to have an abortion and her doctor agrees to it, should she be allowed to have an abortion or not?"

Rephrased more specifically, the question received a different response. To the question "Should abortion be as legal as it is now, or legal only in such cases as rape, incest or to save the life of the mother, or should it not be permitted at all?" only 46 percent said it should be as legal as it is now. Forty-one percent said it should be legal only in such cases as rape or incest or to save the life of the mother. Nine percent said it should not be legal at all.

Polls taken in the five years prior to *Roe* v. *Wade*, when many states were liberalizing their laws on abortion, indicate a far more permissive attitude than those conducted after the landmark decision. The past seven years show significant declines in support for legalized abortion.

This conclusion was drawn by the National Opinion Research Center, a nonprofit polling organization affiliated with the University of Chicago. Experts there say they cannot qualify the public's reasoning.

Polling experts agree that people are more likely to say they favor abortion rights when the question is framed in terms of a "woman's right to choose" than when the question talks about "protecting an unborn child."

The issue continues to be confused even when the right to choose and the rights of the unborn are not juxtaposed.

In the same independent June 1991 Gallup poll that found 82 percent of the public supporting some form of abortion rights, 42 percent responded that they would like to see *Roe* v. *Wade* overturned, a jump of 8 percent from 1989, immediately post-Webster. In the 1991 poll, 66 percent opposed the Rust v. Sullivan ruling and an equally high percentage (66 percent) supported congressional action to overturn the regulation, which bars family planning clinics that receive federal money from providing patients with any information about abortion.

Inconsistencies are more subtle though still apparent throughout the Americans United for Life/Gallup poll administered in February 1991. The poll posed two hundred questions, about two thirds of which pertained to abortion. The following are examples of discrepancies that developed over the course of the survey.

Question 22 C) Is abortion acceptable or unacceptable if there is a strong chance of serious deformity in the baby?

Acceptable during first three months: 58.4%

Acceptable after three months: 41.4%

(Some of the original 58.4% are included in the second figure.)

Question 30 E) New technologies make it possible to discover many things about the unborn early in the pregnancy. Please state which statement best describes your feelings if the baby will be born blind:

Would definitely not consider an abortion   56.1%

Question 30 F) If the baby will be missing an arm or a leg:
Would definitely not consider an abortion   53.3%

Question 32) State whether or not you think it should be possible for a pregnant woman to obtain a legal abortion if there is a strong chance of serious defect in the baby.

Yes	*60.9%*
No	*29.1%*
Don't Know	*9.9%*

With regard to quality of life, please note these responses:

Question 26) Do you strongly agree, agree, disagree, or strongly disagree that the quality of the life of a child will have after it is born is an important thing to consider when deciding on an abortion?

Strongly Agree	*15.8%*
Agree	*34.2%*
Disagree	*27.1%*
Strongly Disagree	*4.6%*

In the above question, 50 percent of respondents strongly agree or agree that quality of life is an important consideration when deciding on an abortion. Yet when asked directly about those factors that might hinder a child's quality of life in relation to the acceptability of abortion, the response is less supportive of abortion.

Here is the breakdown:

Sixty-six percent said that abortion was unacceptable in the first three months if the pregnancy forced a teenager to drop out of school; 66.3 percent said abortion was unacceptable in the first three months if the family has a very low income and another child would create a heavy financial burden; 67.9 percent said abortion was unacceptable in the first three months if the woman has been abandoned by her partner, the father of the unborn child.

Further intra-poll inconsistency exists within the Wirthlin poll, conducted in November 1990, on behalf of the United States Catholic Conference. The six-part poll was intended to assess the following: Americans' knowledge of abortion; Americans' position on abortion, parental consent, information distribution about fetal development and alternatives to abortion before having the procedure, the basic right to life and whether all human life, including that of the unborn, should be protected.

The results to the general question of abortion are as follows: 14 percent said it should be legal only to save the life of the mother; 35 percent, in cases of rape, incest, and to save the life of the mother; 27 percent, for any reason, but not after first three months of pregnancy; 7 percent, legal at any time during pregnancy and for any reason, and 7 percent said abortion should be prohibited in all circumstances. In total, 83 percent of all respondents support some sort of abortion rights, though only 35 percent support such rights under fairly lenient circumstances.

The reaction was different when this statement was posed: "All human life, including that of the unborn, should be protected."

Thirty-one percent said that statement was extremely convincing; 29 percent said it was very convincing; 22 percent said it was not very convincing, and 11 percent said it was not at all convincing. Two percent didn't know and one percent refused to answer. In total, 60 percent were convinced to some degree that the life of an unborn child should be protected.

The response was nearly identical to this statement: "Every unborn child has a basic right to life."

Thirty-two percent said that statement was extremely convincing; 28 percent said it was very convincing; 26 percent said it was not very convincing; 11 percent said it was not at all convincing. One percent didn't know and one percent refused to answer. Again, 60 percent agreed that every unborn child has a basic right to life, although 83 percent of the same respondents said that abortion should be available under certain conditions.

Selected Bibliography

AHLSTROM, SYDNEY E. *A Religious History of the American People*. New Haven, Conn.: Yale University Press, 1972.

BERCOVITCH, SACRAN. *The Puritan Origins of the American Self*. New Haven, Conn.: Yale University Press, 1975.

BONAVOGLIA, ANGELA, ed. *The Choices We Made: Twenty-Five Women Speak Out About Abortion*. New York: Random House, 1991.

CARRICK, PAUL. *Medical Ethics in Antiquity: Philosophical Perspectives on Abortion and Euthanasia*. Kluwer Academic Publishers, 1985.

COATES, JENNIFER. "A Comparison of United States and Canadian Approaches to the Rights of Privacy and Abortion." *Brooklyn Journal of International Law*, Volume XV, No. 3, 1989.

CONNERY, JOHN. *Abortion: The Development of the Roman Catholic Perspective*. Chicago: Loyola University Press, 1977.

D'EMILIO, JOHN, and ESTELLE B. FREEDMAN. *Intimate Matters: A History of Sexuality in America*. New York: Harper and Row, 1988.

DEVEREAUX, GEORGE. *A Study of Abortion in Primitive Societies*. New York: Julian Press, 1955.

FAUST, CLARENCE H., and THOMAS H. JOHNSON. *Jonathan Edwards*. New York: Hill and Wang, 1935.

FELDMAN, DR. DAVID. *Birth Control in Jewish Law*. New York: New York University Press, 1968.

GAMMON, CATHERINE. "Whose Choice?" *Present Tense*, Sept.–Oct. 1989, volume 16, no. 6.

GIRARD, RENÉ. *Violence and the Sacred*. Baltimore: Johns Hopkins University Press, 1972.

GLENDON, MARY ANN. *Abortion and Divorce in Western Law*. Cambridge, Mass.: Harvard University Press, 1987.

GORMAN, MICHAEL J. *Abortion and the Early Church: Christian, Jewish and Pagan Attitudes in the Greco-Roman World*. Intervarsity Press, 1982.

GRISEZ, GERMAIN. *Abortion: The Myths, the Realities, and the Arguments*. New York: Corpus Books, 1970.

HASTINGS, JAMES, ed. *Encyclopedia of Religion and Ethics*. New York: Scribner's, 1961.

HODGSON, GODFREY. *America in Our Time*. New York: Vintage (Random House), 1976.

HUSER, ROGER. *The Crime of Abortion in Canon Law*. Washington, D.C.: Catholic University Press, 1942.

KAZIN, ALFRED, and DANIEL AARON, ed. *Emerson: A Modern Anthology*. New York: Dell, 1958.

LUKER, KRISTIN. *Abortion and the Politics of Motherhood*. Berkeley and Los Angeles: University of California Press, 1984.

MARTY, MARTIN. *Righteous Empire*. New York: Dial Press, 1970.

MAY, HENRY F. *The Enlightenment in America*. New York: Oxford University Press, 1976.

MILLER, PERRY, ed. *American Thought: Civil War to World War I*. New York: Holt, Rinehart and Winston, 1962.

————. *Errand Into the Wilderness*. Cambridge, Mass.: Harvard University Press, 1956.

MOHR, JAMES C. "The Historical Character of Abortion in the United States," in Paul Sachdev, *Perspectives on Abortion*. Metuchen, N.J.: Scarecrow Press, Inc., 1985.

NOONAN, JOHN. *Contraception: A History of Its Treatment by Catholic Theologians and Canonists*. Cambridge, Mass.: Harvard University Press, 1965.

————, ed. *The Morality of Abortion: Legal and Historical Perspectives*. Cambridge, Mass.: Harvard University Press, 1970.

POTTS, MALCOLM. "Intellectual History of Abortion," in Paul Sachdev, *Perspectives on Abortion*. Metuchen, N.J.: Scarecrow Press, Inc., 1985.

PRITCHARD, JAMES B., ed. *Ancient Near Eastern Texts Relating to the Old Testament*. Princeton, N.J.: Princeton University Press, 1955.

RABB, THEODORE K., and ROBERT I. ROTBERG. *The Family in History*. New York: Harper and Row, 1971.

SLOTKIN, RICHARD. *Regeneration Through Violence: The Mythology of the American Frontier, 1600–1860*. Middletown, Conn.: Wesleyan University Press, 1973.

TOCQUEVILLE, ALEXIS DE. *Democracy in America*. Garden City, N.Y.: Doubleday, 1969.

TRILLING, LIONEL. *The Liberal Imagination*. Garden City, N.Y.: Doubleday, 1950.

TRIBE, LAURENCE H. *Abortion: The Clash of Absolutes*. London: Norton & Co., 1990.

TURNER, FREDERICH JACKSON. *The Frontier in American History*. New York: Holt, Rinehart and Winston, 1962.

WILLS, GARRY. *Under God: Religion and American Politics*. New York: Simon & Schuster, 1960.